Microsoft Word 2010 level 2   unit standard 117924

The training material is aligned to the unit standard 117924 and after completing the studying of this training material you will be well prepared to pass exam 117924

This manual is designed for class room training, one on one coaching or self-learning.

Word processing principles   Level 2

- Working with multiple documents
- Advanced formatting
- Tabs
- Numbering
- Footnotes and end notes
- Creating and formatting tables
- Inserting pictures & objects
- Headers and footers
- Page layout functions
- Creating and Formatting columns
- Linking Word and Excel
- Creating an using Templates
- Translation to French or Spanish
- Advanced printing

Microsoft Word 2010 Training Manual level 2

About this manual

This training manual is designed by YolandieMostert and are copyright protected.
No copies are allowed without the written permission of the author

The following are used <> to indicate to either type in a word or select a menu item, at no point must you type in <> especialy not when your saving files

> ➤ This icon ,the arrow key in front of this line, indicates a list of instructions to follow

> ↓ The preceding icon is indicative of optional instructions

There are practical exercises that is recommended for your to complete during each module

There is an estimated time period in which you could complete the modules however you could be able to complete it in a shorter time or you could take a little bit longer. Each person are unique and have there own pace to work on.. It is recommended that you do some more exercises after the first day of training.

There is also additional exercises at the end of this manual that you can complete at your own perusal or on the instructions of your trainer. Do as many exercises until you feel comfortable.

After you studied this manual, you can go to any training organization that have accredited evaluators to evaluate you, when they found you competent in theory and practise of this training material you can earn credits towards a qualification of your choice. The training material is aligned to the SAQA Exams, and thus you only have to study what is in this manual to get your credits for Exam 117924 The SAQA :Exam questionnaire is available to download for free on the internet.

The unit standard for above information may differ in your country.

After completing this training material you will be able to master the contents of above information and pass any exam that will be testing above information.

Should you wish to order more training material please. Email: Quality1Training@gmail.com You are also welcome to call if you wish to make bookings for personal or group training.

Yolandie Mostert trained thousands of students in spreadsheet programs, word programs and windows programs. She will enjoy training you. However the manuals are well explained and therefor you can train yourself with this training material, without a tutor.

Any other training material can be designed for you on request, please call above contact number if you want any other training material. Microsoft PowerPoint and Microsoft Excel training material is also available.

Copyright© 2014 by Yolandie Mostert You will need written permission to make extra copies from this book.

Microsoft Word 2010 Training Manual level 2

Working with multiple documents

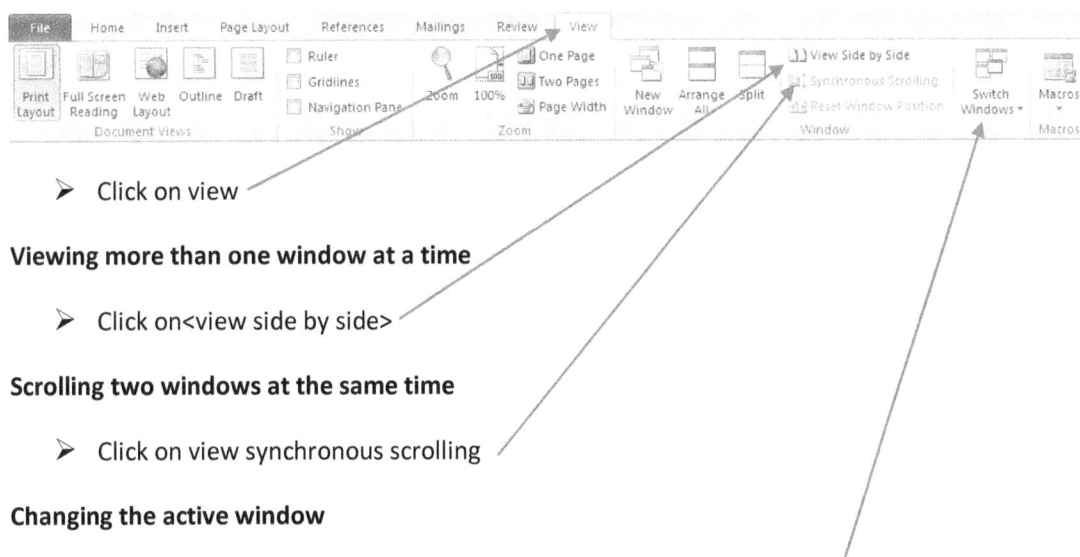

- Click on view

Viewing more than one window at a time

- Click on <view side by side>

Scrolling two windows at the same time

- Click on view synchronous scrolling

Changing the active window

- Click on switch windows, select the document you want to work on

Viewing all active windows

- Click on arrange all

Zoom

Enlarging a document or decreasing the viewing size

- Click on zoom

- Click on the up or down arrow to increase or decrease the percentage.

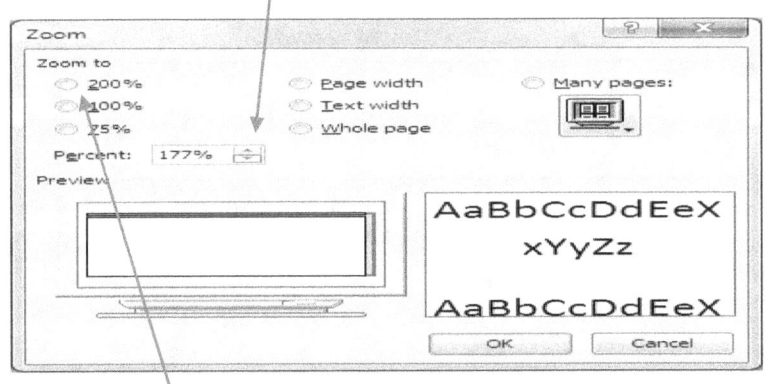

- Click inside the circle next to 200% to make the letters twice as large or

- Click inside the circle next to 75% to make the letters smaller

Viewing gridlines

Gridlines are vertical and horizontal lines inside the document, you can switch them on or off

- Click inside the checkbox, located at the view tab, to activate the gridlines

Tab stops

You can create your own tab stops in MS Word. The data will be aligned at each tab stop
Notice on the left side of the ruler appears the left alignment tab stop, that is active by default.
- Clicking on this tab stop will change it to either right alignment or centre alignment

How to create a tab stop with the ruler:
- Choose an area on the ruler where you wish to set a tab stop.
- Click on the area on the ruler where you wish to put the tab stop.
- You can place as many tab stops that you want, just click on the number where you want it.

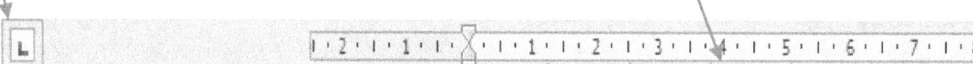

Practise exercise tab stops
- Click on the ruler on number 4 and number 10, at the bottom of the number on the ruler

The tab stops are now set at 4 and 10 indicated by the L on the ruler, ready for you to enter data

Practical exercise to enter data, using the above tab stops

- Press the enter key to start a new line
- Type the following < Name>
- Press the tab key once
- Type the following <Surname>
- Press the tab key once
- Type the following <Telephone number>
- Press enter
- Type the following <Yolandie>
- Press tab once
- Type "Mostert"
- Press tab once
- Type +27797772857
- Press enter
- Type your name surname and telephone number by following above example
- Type your friends details by following the same example
- Save the document

Removing tab stops
If you no longer wish to have tab stops

- Click on <clear Formatting> on the menu, to remove all the tab stops

Removing a specific Tab stop

- Click on the tab stop and hold down the left button and drag it down from the ruler

Method 2   Setting tab stops using the tabs dialog box

- Right click to get the short cut menu and select the paragraph option
- Click on tabs, on the left bottom corner of the paragraph dialog box

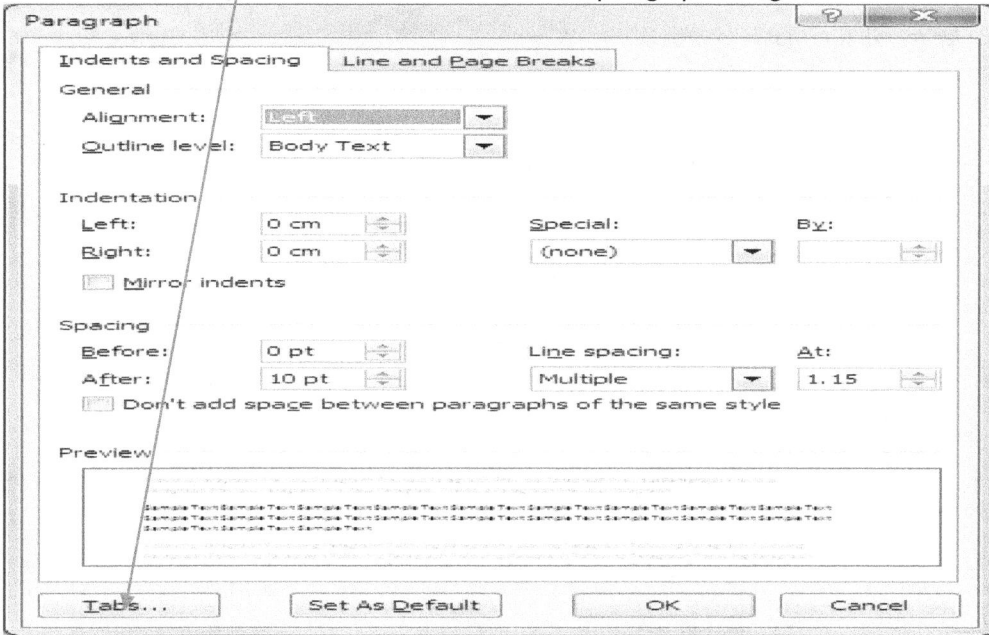

The tabs dialog box appear

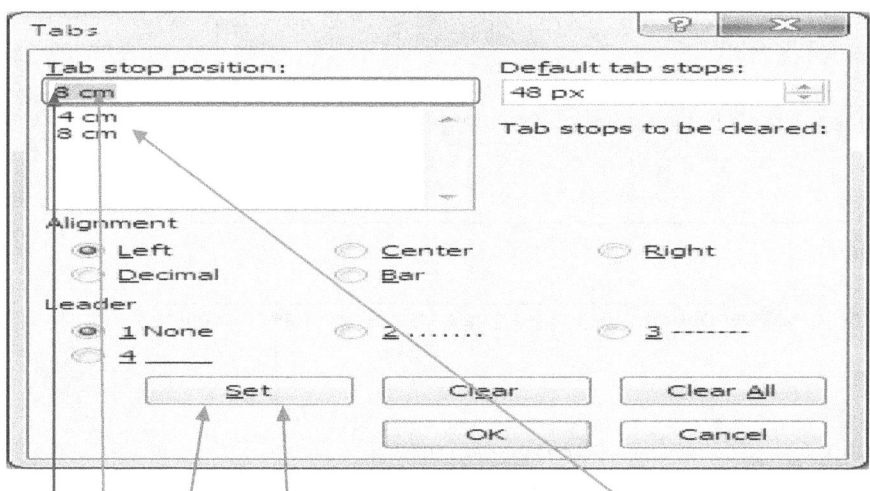

Practical exercise: Creating tab stops at 4 and 8 cm by using the tabs dialog box

- Type in the tab stop position inside the white rectangle, at the top left of the tabs window
- *Click inside the white rectangle and type 8,* this is the number that will be visible on the ruler
- Click on set, once you click on set, the number will be visible in this white square
- Type in the next tab stop inside the white rectangle, at the top left of the tabs window
- *Type 4   ,Click on set,*
- Click on ok
  The tab stops is automaticaly inserted onto the ruler once you click on <ok>

Notice above there are now a tab stop at the number 4 and 8

Microsoft Word 2010 Training Manual level 2

Leader tab stops.

A leader tab stop is when special characters are created between the tab stops

Notice the example of a dot leader tab stop that follows below:

Exercise leader tab stop

- Activate the tab dialog box (refer to previous page on how to do this)

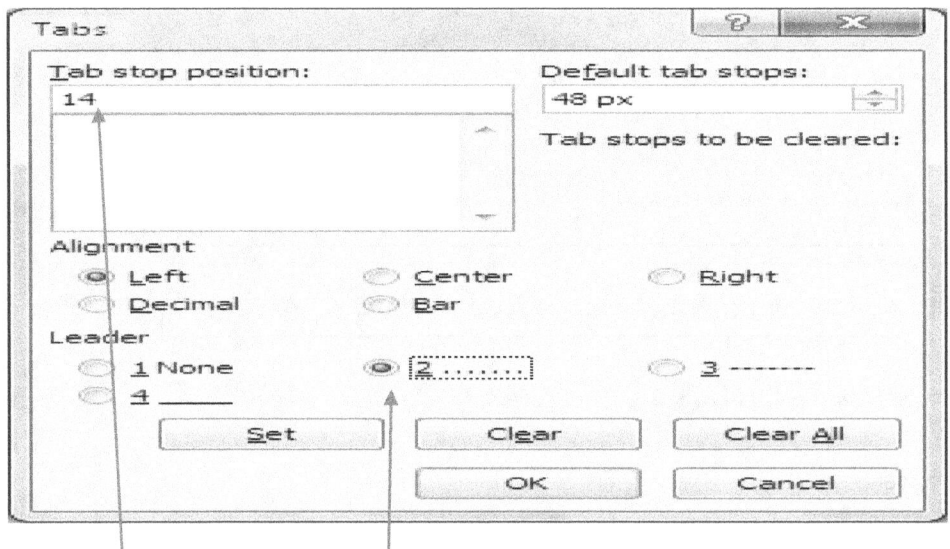

- At the tab stop position type in 14
- At the leader, click inside the radio button number 2 so that leading dots will appear
- Click on ok
- Press enter for a new line
- Press the <tab key> type in number one, notice the leading dots that appear on the line
- and Press enter
- Press the <tab key> notice again the leading dots, type in number 2

Result of exercise below showing the leading dots:

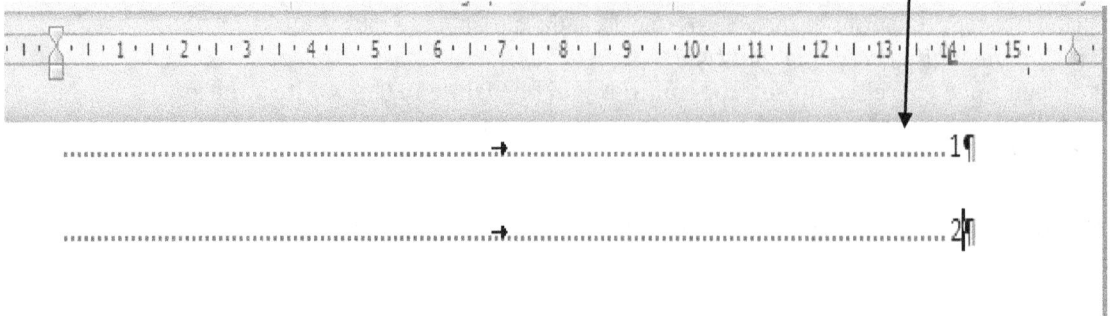

Microsoft Word 2010 Training Manual level 2

Creating vertical lines between tab stops

- Activate the tab dialog box
- At the alignment option, click until you see the following icon I, which is the bar icon

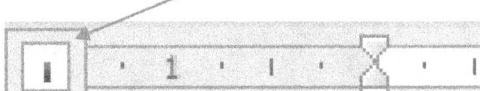

- Then click on the ruler where you want the verticle lines to appear

Example below : the tab stop has been set on 2 cm and 4 cm and 8 cm

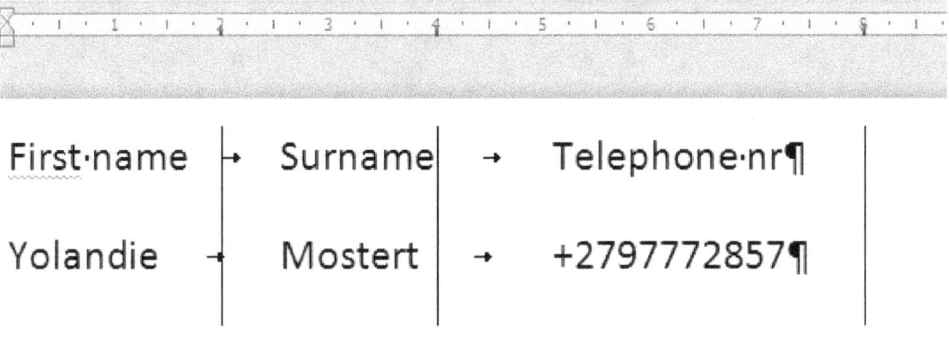

Hyphenation

Hyphenation is when a word is broken up into 2 pieces at the end of the line, when it doesn't fit on-to the line.

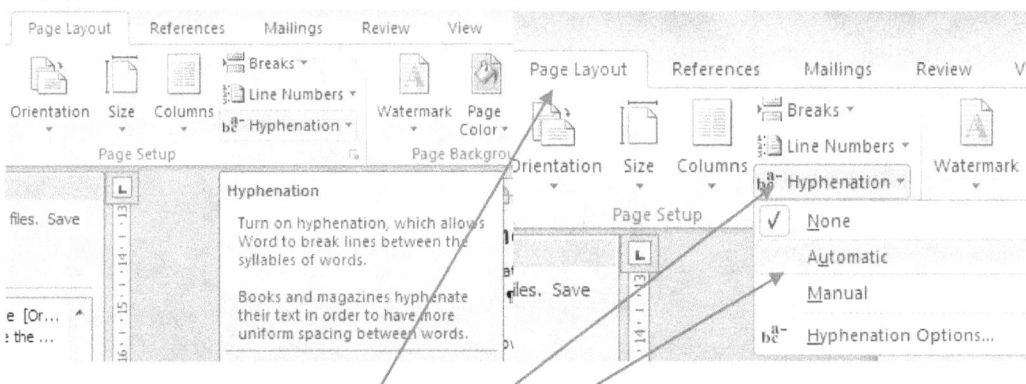

The following character <-> called a hyphen are added

- Click on page layout
- Click on hyphenation
- Select automatic

*Manual hyphenations: Ctrl + - breaks the word and control +shift+- keep the word together

Microsoft Word 2010 Training Manual level 2

Advanced Formatting   60 min

After the training session you will be able to:

> ➢ **Use styles**
> ➢ **Create new styles**
> ➢ **Apply Number formatting**
> ➢ **Create Paragraph formatting**

Using existing styles

Styles are the combined format, for example **bold** and 12 font and Underlined

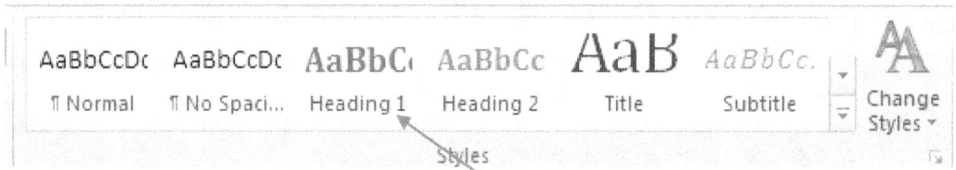

By clicking on any of the styles above you will be applying that style format to your active paragraph, for example if heading one is blue and 14 font and bold, the paragraph will be formatted with those attributes.

> ➢ Click anywhere in the paragraph that you want to apply a style to
> ➢ Click on the formatting style of your choice, for example <heading 1>

Creating new styles

You can also create your own styles

You can select any of the existing styles and then make changes to it and save it as a new style with a new name that you can use whenever you want to.

For this practical example

> ➢ click on heading 1 and
> ➢ Next to the title style click on the bottom down arrow

The following screen will appear:

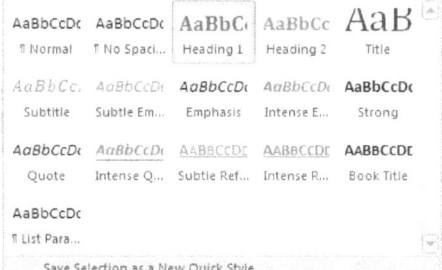

Click on <save selection as a new quick style>

The following screen will appear:

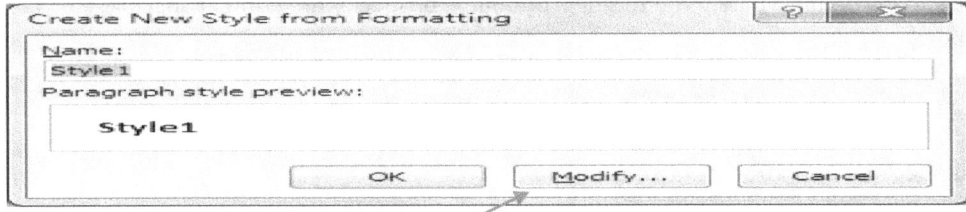

Type in a name for your new style, if you don't type in a new name the name of your style will be saved as style1.

> Click on modify, the following screen will appear:

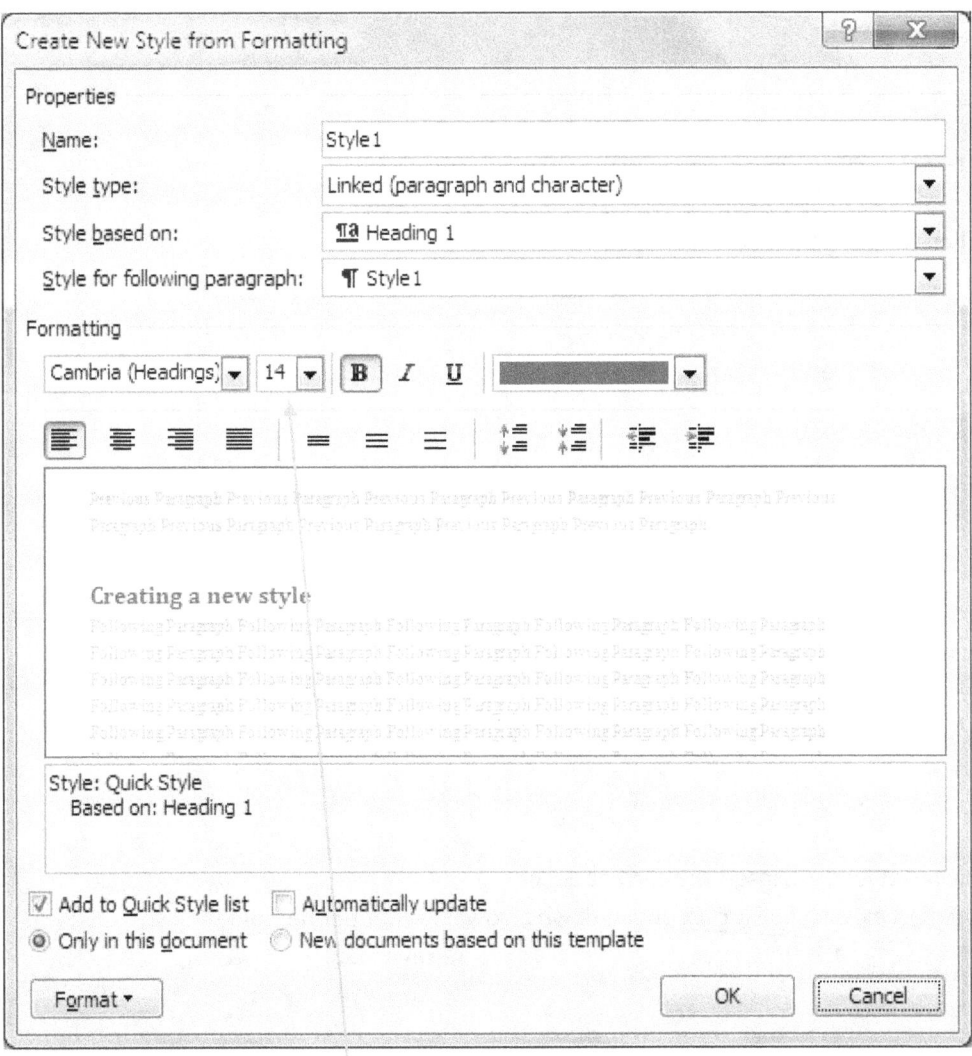

For this practical example, we will change the font size of the new style to 18

Changing the font style

> Click on the down arrow next to the number 14 and select 18

> Click on <ok> your new style should now be listed

Microsoft Word 2010 Training Manual level 2

Paragraph formatting

You can adjust the line spacing within a paragraph to single or double or specify the number spacing before and after the line.

- Select a paragraph
- Right click and select paragraph
- Or click on paragraph formatting on the ribbon menu-->

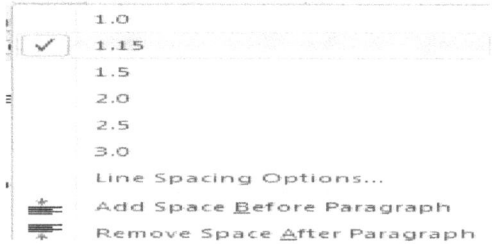

The following screens will appear when you click on above paragraph formatting option on the ribbon:

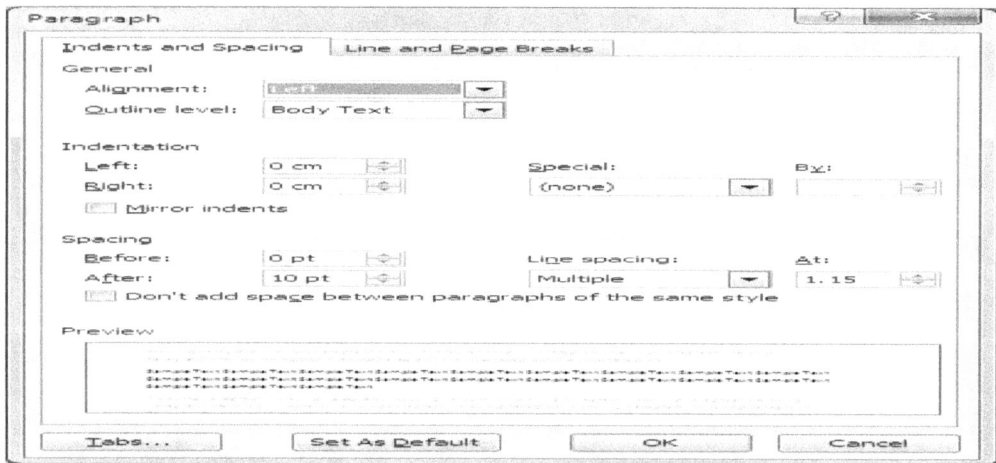

Line space options when selecting the option paragraph on the short cut menu:

Adding bullets

- Clicking on the bullet icon will insert the current bullet
- To insert a different existing bullet click on the down arrow and choose one from the list

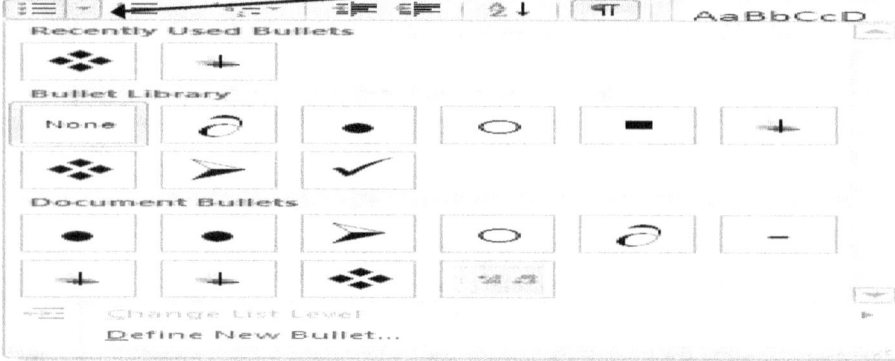

➢ Click on define new bullet to create a new bullet

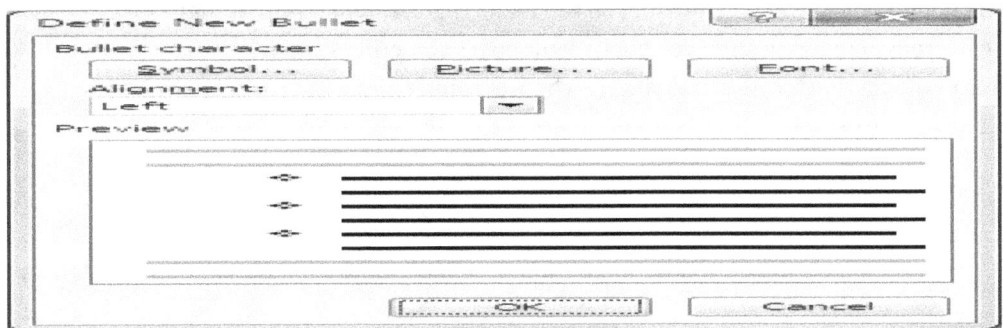

clicking on symbol will provide the following dialog box

Clicking on pictureto insert a picture

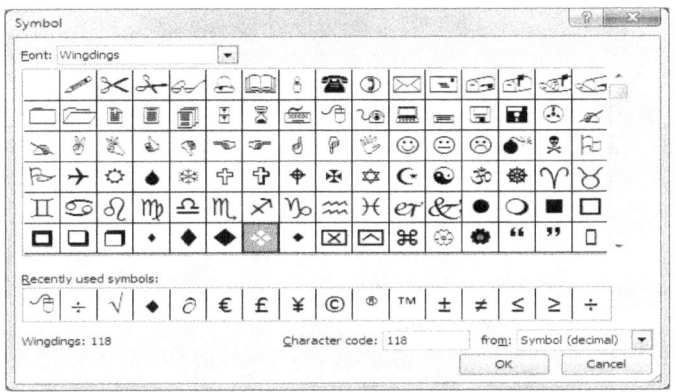
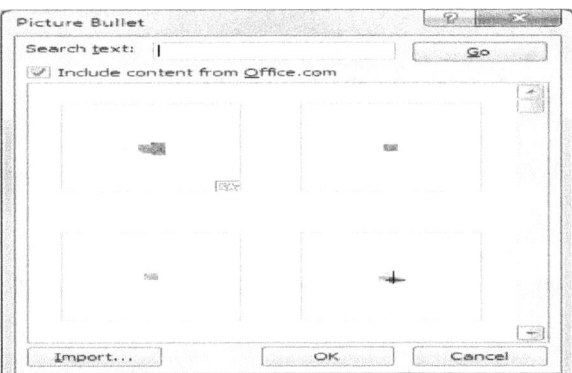

Alignment of bullets

Notice on the ruler where the starting point of the bullet is and where the starting point of the sentence is. The starting point of the bullet is on the first line indent. The starting point on the text is on the hanging indent. If you wish to change the space between the bullet and the text, move the hanging indent on the ruler. If you wish to move the bullet, move the first line indent on the ruler

Removing bullets

➢ Press the backspace key to remove a bullet or

➢ Select the bullets you wish to remove and press delete

➢ Or when you create a list of bullets and you press enter, the bullet for the next line will disappear

Number formatting

If you wish to use numbering in your document, you can make changes to the format that you want to use for your numbering and even create your own numbering system

Examples of numbering formats that you can choose from:

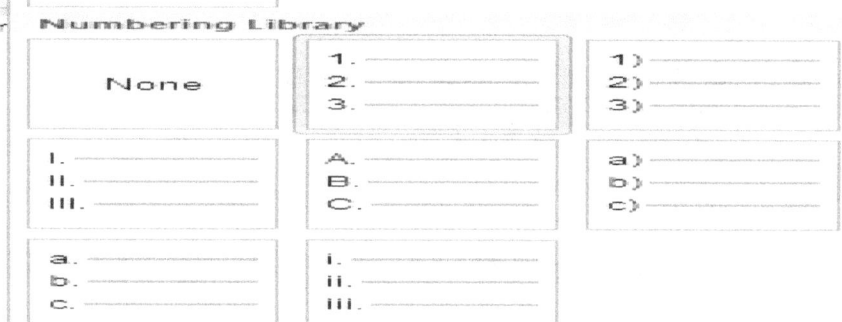

Example of a numbering system:

Notice in this example below the first level is numbers 1,2,3 the second level is a,b,c and third level is I,ii,

1) Hello, My name is Yolandie, I am the author of this manual, please do not make copies of these manuals illegally, since I sell the training manuals in order to have food to eat .
2) I have worked hard on these manuals and will appreciate your assistance to ensure that people do not make illegal copies of my material, since I use the funds also to help less privileged people
    a) Poor doggies and kittens will starve of hunger if I don't generate funds from these books
    b) Please report people that make illegal copies of my material
        i) You can call me at +27797772857
    c) I really appreciate your help
    d) Thank you
3) Sincerely from Yolandie Mostert

How to start numbering using an existing numbering system:

1. Click on numbering to start the number list
2. From the numbering library select the first numbering system
    a. This numbering list have the following levels, level 1 = 1,2.,3.. level 2 = abc.. level 3 = I, ii,iii,iv.
    b. Each level have an indentation of 1.27cm
        i. **Press the tab key to move to the next level**
        ii. **Press the shift tab key to move back one level**
3. *Pressing shift tab changed this line from a iv, to a "c" to a 3*
4. *When you press enter you get the next line*

The cursor must be next to the number or letter when you press tab or shift tab, or enter.
Practise exercise: *Use the numbering list above and type in the data above, on how to create a new list*

Microsoft Word 2010 Training Manual level 2

Create a new number list, directly after the previous one
When you want to start a new numbering list, directly after the previous one, you can use this option. The cursor have to be on an existing list , for this function to be active.

- ➢ Click on the down arrow next to numbering, 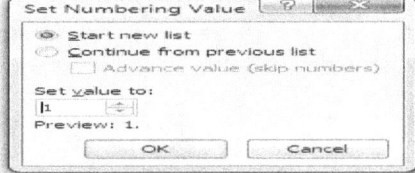 on the top menu in the left middle.
- ➢ Click on <**set number value**> the last option on this menu.
- ➢ Make sure that the option <start a new list> have a blue dot inside, if it doesn't, click inside the little white circle, to activate this option.
- ➢ Click on the up or down arrow to set the value to a desired number, the existing value will change to the number of your choice, and the next row will continue with the new numbering list.
- ➢ *Below is an example of 2 lists that have been created with this function*

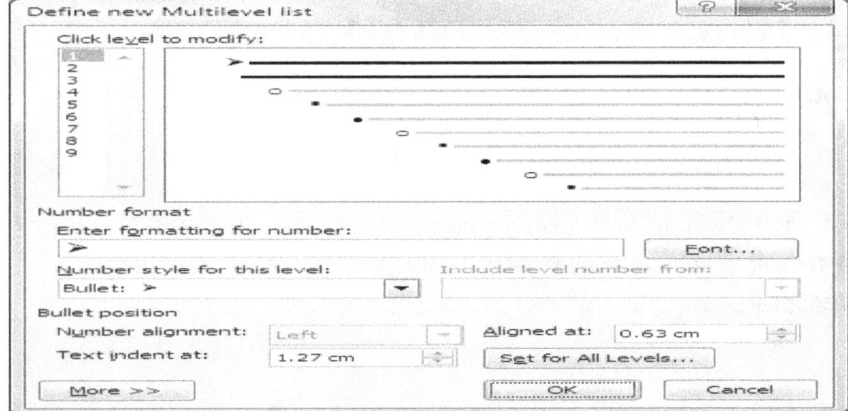

Practise exercise: Create the sample above, with 3 numbers repeating
We will first create the first list, by
- ➢ Selecting numbering and choosing the first list option in the library
- ➢ Press enter twice to create number 2 and 3, you must type data next to the numbers otherwise the numbering list will stop the numbering.
- ➢ Press the enter key once more for number 4
- ➢ Click on the down arrow next to numbering and
- ➢ choose <set number value> click on the down arrow change the 4 into a 1

The number 4 will now change into a 1 and the next number will be a 2 and thereafter a 3 will appear

Creating your own multi level list (Creating your own number formatting levels)
- ➢ Click on multi level list on the top menu, in the middle
- ➢ Click on define new multi level list ,the second last option on this menu
- ➢ The following menu will appear, click on each level number and choose the character for that level, you can also choose to include the previous level number for example 1.1
- ➢ Like the example below, you can choose bullets or numbers for your numbering list

- ➢ Click on the down arrow at <number style for this level> and select number or bullets

Footnotes and Endnotes

[1]Footnotes are usually used to explain information about a paragraph or word. And are available at the end of a page. Footnotes – Press CTRL ALT F

Below is a print screen of the bottom of a page, since remember footnotes appear at the end of a page

> **Footnotes**
>
> ➤ Click on Reference, Insert Footnote
>
> A footnote [1] is a note you attach to a specific word, to give more detai[2]ls on that specific word.
>
> The footnote will appear at the end of the page with a reference number ontop of the word.
>
> Where ever the cursor is, is where the footnote will appear in the document. Click in front of the word, that you want to add a footnote too, if you wish the number to appear in front of the word.
>
> Foot notes will automatically be renumbered.
>
> ---
> [1] This is a footnote explaining how it works, this is the first footnote
> [2] This is the second footnote, to explain how it works

When adding a footnote, a little number will appear on top of the word, that will be explained at the bottom of the page.

End notes

[i]End notes appear at the end of a document, and are also used for reference in paragraphs and also get renumbered when you add extra endnotes to a document.

Notice that a endnote has been placed on the word <endnote> at the beginning of above paragraph, a small >i> appear on top of the word, indicating the end note reference, you will find the explanation of the endnote at the end of this manual, since remember end notes are similar to footnotes the difference is that endnotes appear at the end of a document.

➤ Click on Reference, Insert Endnote   Or press – Press CTRL ALT D

Deleting footnotes and endnotes

Select the reference number that is inside the document and press delete on the keyboard.

You don't select the endnote or footnote at the bottom of the page, you simply select the little number that is inserted inside the paragraphs and once that is deleted the endnote or footnote at the bottom of the page will disappear

---

[1] This is another example of a footnote, notice that footnotes appear at the end of a page.

Microsoft Word 2010 Training Manual level 2

Tables   60 min

Creating tables

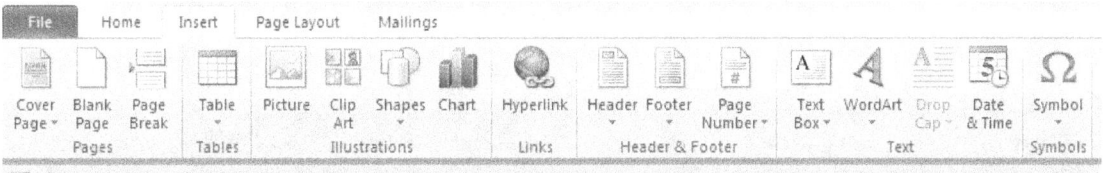

When you wish to add a list of entries for example a telephone or address list it is easier to create a table and add the entries to a table. A table exist of rows and columns and you can add or delete borderlines and shading to the table

How to insert a table

- Click on insert Table

(there are 4 ways of creating a table)

- Insert table by selecting blocks
- Insert table by typing in number of rows and columns
- Insert table by drawing it in the document
- Quick access tables

Insert table by selecting blocks

Move the cursor over the tiny square blocks, this will indicate to word how many rows and columns you wish to add to your table, columns are the vertical blocks and rows are the horizontal blocks. The rows and columns that are selected will turn orange and the table will be created inside the document where the active cursor is.

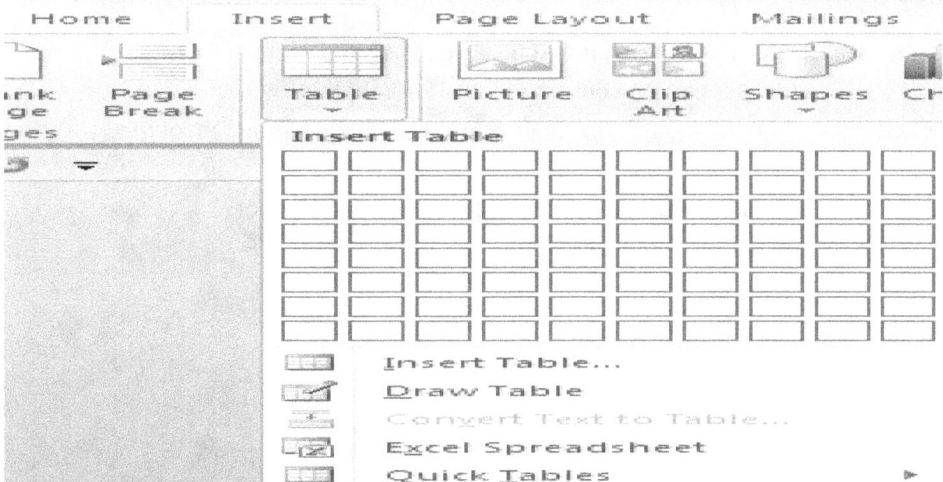

Inserting a table by typing in number of rows and columns

- Click on insert, table,

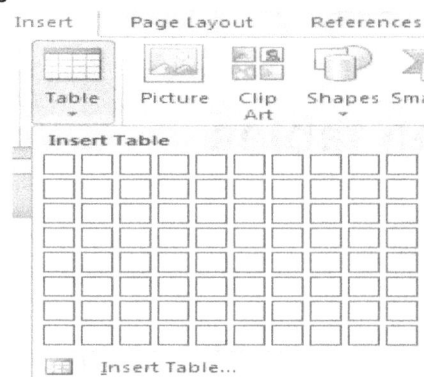

- select <insert table> option →

The following screen will appear:

- Number of columns: Click inside the white square and type in how many columns you wish for your table, or click on the up and down arrow to change the values
- Number of rows: type in how many rows you wish inside the white square, to insert in your table or click on the up and down arrow to change the values
- Click on <ok> to insert the table into the document
- Result of above exercise should look like the following example below:

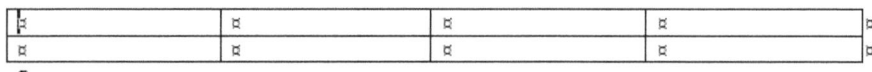

Inserting a table by drawing it in the document

With drawing tables, you have the freedom to create the table into any format of your choice
Below is a practical example of how you can use the drawing table option

Ensure that there is enough space in the document to draw a large square.

- Click on insert , table
- Click on <draw table> and draw a large square into your document (notice a little pencil appears on your screen to draw your table
- Now add the horizontal lines by dragging the pencil from the left margin of the square to the right margin of the square.
- Also add the vertical line by dragging the pencil from top to bottom

Below is an example of what it could look like:

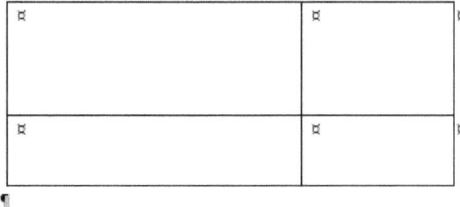

Quick access tables

With quick access tables, the rows and columns have already been added, and formatting has been applied, you will also be inserting pre-existing data into your document that you can change.

How to create a quick access table
- Click on ,Insert table, Quick tables
- Select the option that you want from the list, click on the up and down arrow to scroll through the list options,
- Click on the option that you want to insert in the document

For example :

You can select an already made calendar from the list that has been formatted

MAY

M	T	W	T	F	S	S
	1	2	3	4	5	6
7	8	9	10	11	12	13
14	15	16	17	18	19	20
21	22	23	24	25	26	27
28	29	30	31			

You can also insert a sample table of the greek alphabet into your document

The Greek alphabet

Letter name	Uppercase	Lowercase	Letter name	Uppercase	Lowercase
Alpha	A	α	Nu	N	ν
Beta	B	β	Xi	Ξ	ξ
Gamma	Γ	γ	Omicron	O	o
Delta	Δ	δ	Pi	Π	π
Epsilon	E	ε	Rho	P	ρ
Zeta	Z	ζ	Sigma	Σ	σ
Eta	H	η	Tau	T	τ
Theta	Θ	θ	Upsilon	Υ	υ
Iota	I	ι	Phi	Φ	φ
Kappa	K	κ	Chi	X	χ
Lambda	Λ	λ	Psi	Ψ	ψ
Mu	M	μ	Omega	Ω	ω

Inserting an Excel spreadsheet

You can insert a table by using the Excel spreadsheet functions to create the table and then insert the completed table into the word document. With this function you don't need to open MS Excel, the function will provide the Excel functions for you, once you

- ➢ Click on Insert table, Excel spreadsheet
- ➢ A spreadsheet table with 10 rows and 7 columns is visible inside the word document
- ➢ Double click inside the block to start typing in the data
- ➢ Double click inside the table to activate MS Excel and create the table by using the MS Excel features. **Notice at the top, the Excel screen layout appear**, you can now use the Excel autosum to calculate the totals or do any calculations of your choice and format the sheet

name	production
jean	30
jeff	40
johny	50
total	**120**

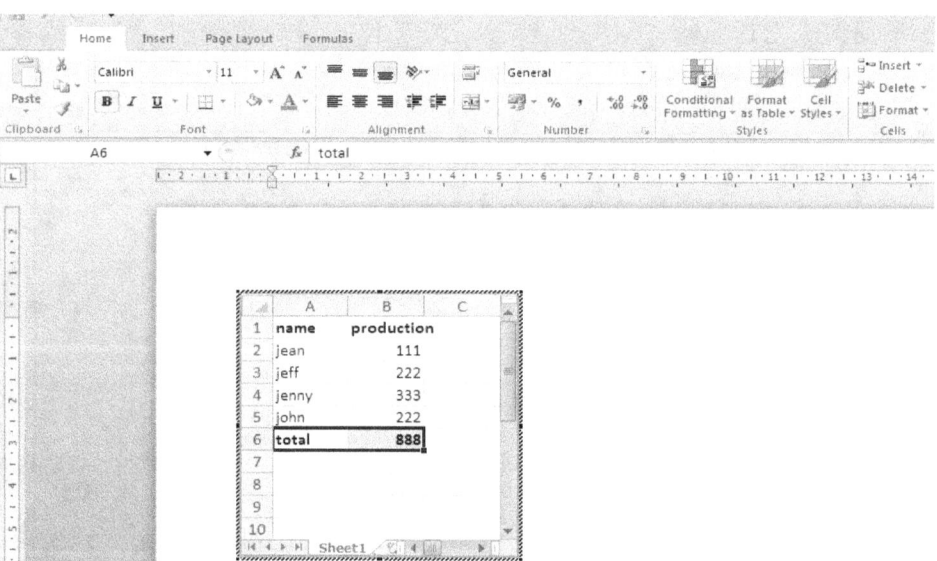

When you have completed adding the data, just click beneath the excel sheet, to return to MS Word, and have the sheet inserted into the word document.

Resizing the table
You can resize the Excel table to ensure that extra columns are not inserted into the word document

- ➢ Move the cursor to the border of the Excel table and once you see the line with the 2 arrows, hold down the left mouse button and drag the cursor to the left to decrease the number of columns that will be inserted into the document

Formatting tables in MS Word

You can add color into your table and choose different styles for the lines that are drawn in the table

- Click anywhere inside the table that you want to format
- Click on <design> on the menu at the top

    This option is not available if you don't click inside a table

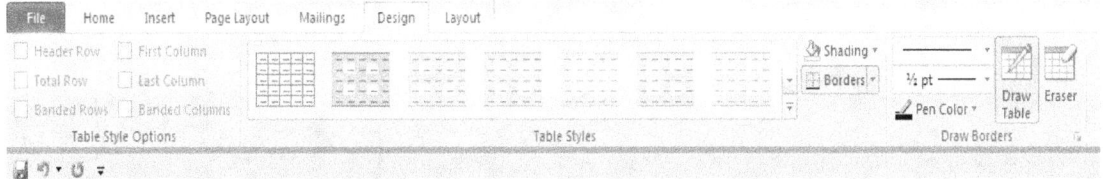

You can choose from a list of pre-existing styles or create your own

Selecting a table style

In the ribbon menu, at the top , in the center, is a list of pre-existing table styles.

- Click on any one of those styles to apply them into your table
- Next to the visible table styles is a down arrow, if you click on it ,it will present more styles that you can select

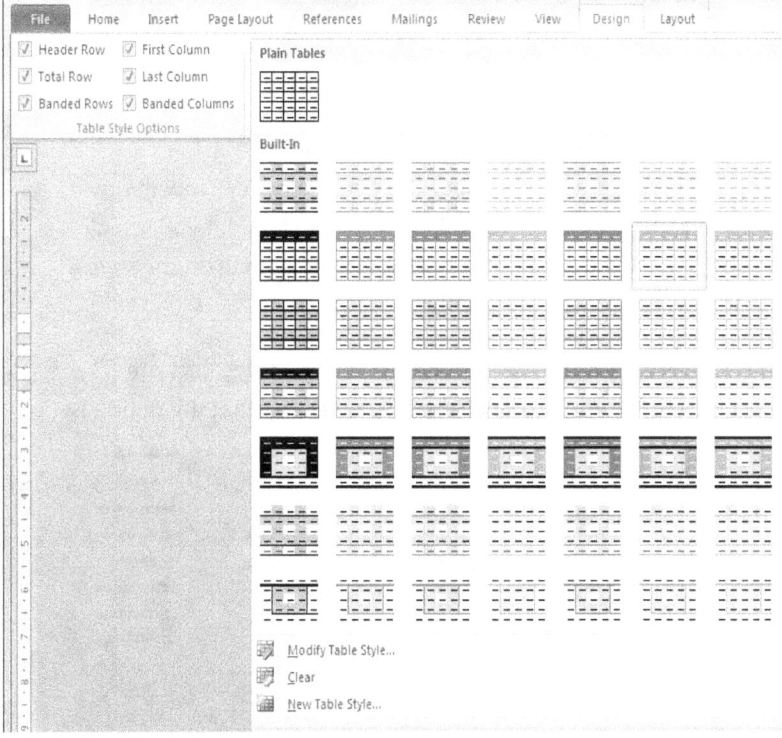

- Click on <new table style> if you want to create your own table style that you want to use later

When you click on new table style, the following screen appears

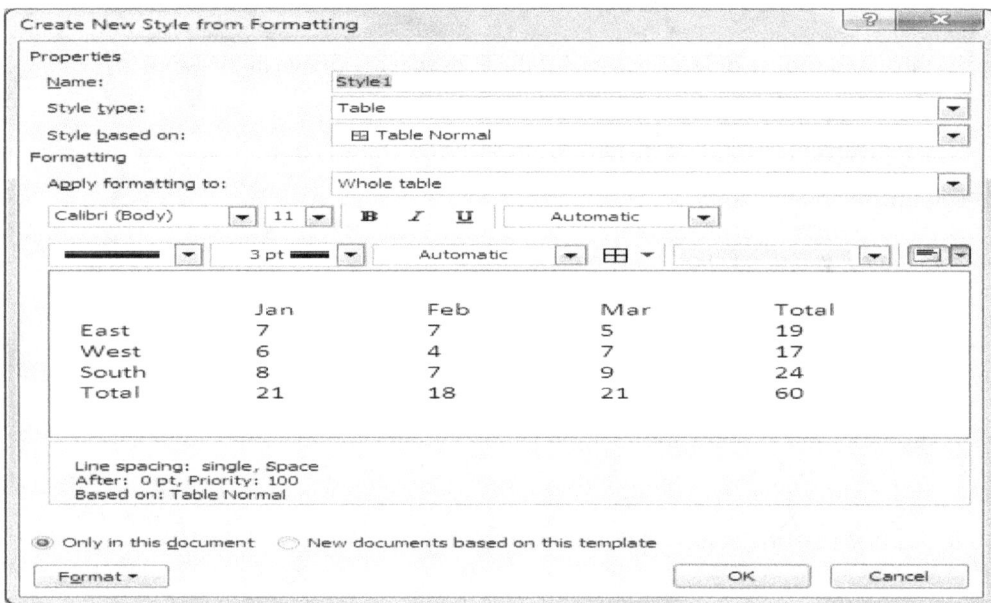

- Type in a name for your new style
- Click on the down arrows to change the existing style and create your own design.

On the left side of the screen you can make more changes to the style

By clicking inside the little squares you will indicate wheather your table havea header row that will be underlined or shaded in most styles and a first column that will be formatted bold.If you select the total row, the second last line will be underlined or double underlined, depending on the style type. Banded rows or columns will shade every second row or column.

When there is a √ inside the little square, it means that that option is selected. To deselect the option click again in the little square and then the √mark will dissapear, indicating that the option is not active.

Making your own design directly into the existing table

Select the area that you want to format
On the rigth side of the style options you will find the shading and border options
Changing the border line style
Next to the shading option is a line, click on the down arrow next to the line to select the line style.

Line weight (thickness of line)

The line next to borders indicate the line weight, the thickness of the line

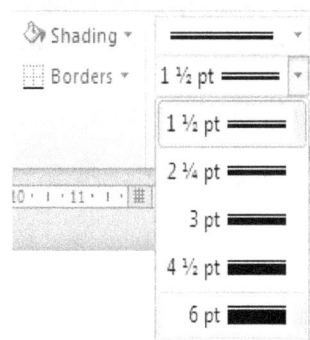

- 1 pt is a very thin line and
- 6 pt is a thick line
  - ➤ Click on the down arrow and select the line weight of your choice

Shading

The shading option is to add colour inside the table

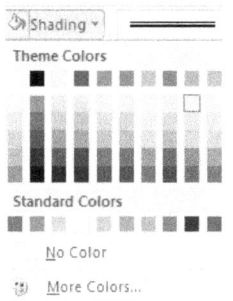

- ➤ Select the area that you want to colour
- ➤ Click on the down arrow next to shading and choose a colour

Draw table

At the right side of the table menu you will notice the draw table option, next to draw table is an eraser, this is how you can delete lines you no longer want.

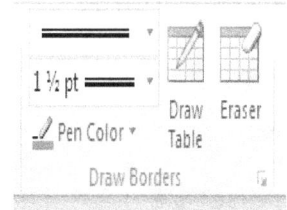

- ➤ Click on draw table icon to draw lines into your table
  The draw table icon should be orange indicating that it is switched on, then a small pencil appear inside the table, with which you can draw the lines
  You can draw horizontal, vertical and diagonal lines
  - ➤ Click on the down arrows next to the lines to change the line style and weight.

Drawing a horizontal line
Click on the left side of the table and hold down the left mouse button while you move the cursor to the right, release the mouse button when you're finished drawing the line.

Erasing a line
- ➤ Click on eraser to delete lines in your table
- ➤ move the eraser over the table line to erase it

Pen color
- ➤ Click on the down arrow to change the color of the line
- ➤ Click on the color of your choice

Adding and Deleting Rows and Columns

On the layout menu you have options to add or delete rows an columns, merge or split cells

- Click inside your table and click on the layout tab at the top menu, on the right

Deleting a row

- Select the rows you want to delete and click on delete on the layout menu on the left top
- Select delete row

Deleting a column

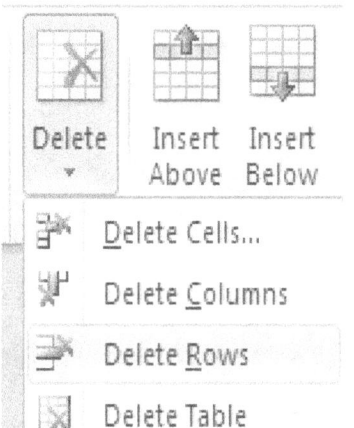

- Click inside the column you want to delete and
- Click on delete on the layout menu
- Select delete columns

Delete Table

You can also delete the whole table

- Click inside the table
- Click on delete
- Click on delete table

Adding Rows

- Click on the row where you want to insert a row below or above
- Click on insert above or if you want a row above the current one or
- Click on insert below if you want to insert a row below the current one

Adding columns

- Click on layout, click on insert left to insert a column to the left of the current collumn
- Click on insert right to insert a column to the right of the current column

Changing the column width and row height

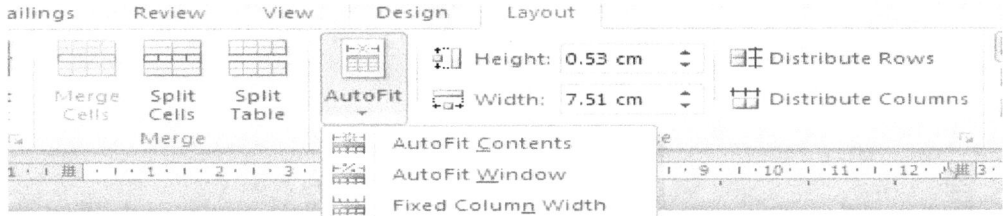

Autofit contents

Autofit contents will find the largest entry in a row and then format the column width to that size

- Click anywhere inside the table, to activate the table
- Click on layout, autofit, select autofit content

Autofit windows

Autofit window, will enlarge the table to fit into the window size

- Click anywhere inside the table, to activate the table
- Click on layout, autofit , select autofit window

Fixed column width

You can define your own width and height

- Click on the up and down arrow next to height and width and select the desired options

Distribute rows and columns

Distributing columns will make each column the same size

Merge cells

You can make two cells one by merging them

- Select the cells you want to merge
- Click on layout, click on merge

Split cells

You can make one cell ,two by splitting them

- Select the cell you want to split and click on split cell

Split Table

You can make one table, two by splitting them

- Click on the row where you want the split to occur
- Click on split table

Creating formulas by using MS Word calculations

If you have a list of items that you want to calculate the totals,

- Ensure you are in the last row where you wish to create totals
- Click on the table layout view and select FX the formula = sum(above) will be added into your table

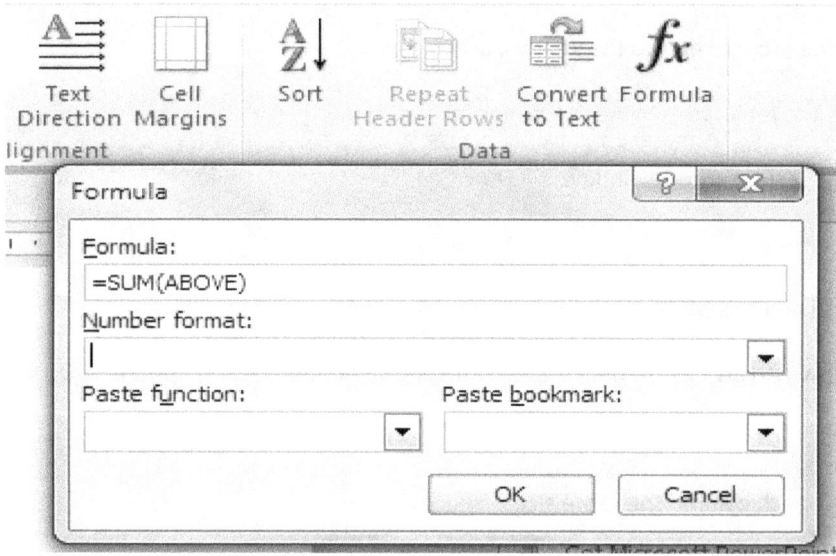

Exercise: create a table with 2 columns and 4 rows

Type in production report and add the totals
(the production values must be in column 2 and names in column 1)
To add the totals, make sure the active cursor is underneath the last value, then click on fx
Production report

Yolandie	100
Jacob	80
Thabo	80
Total production	fx

Aligning text in a table

> Click on layout, and choose the text alignment

Select the data and click on the alignment option of your choice

Top left	Top center	Top right
Center left	center	Center right
Bottom left	Bottom center	Bottom right

Text direction

You can also change the direction of the text
> Click on text direction, more than once and watch how the arrow key change into the a different direction indicating the direction the text will appear inside the table

> Click on layout, text direction

Right by default		Down on first click	UP on second click
Right again on third click		Down again on forth click	Up again on faith click

Cell margins

You can set a top left right and bottom margin for a cell

> Click on layout, click on cell margin, click on the up and down arrows to change the margins

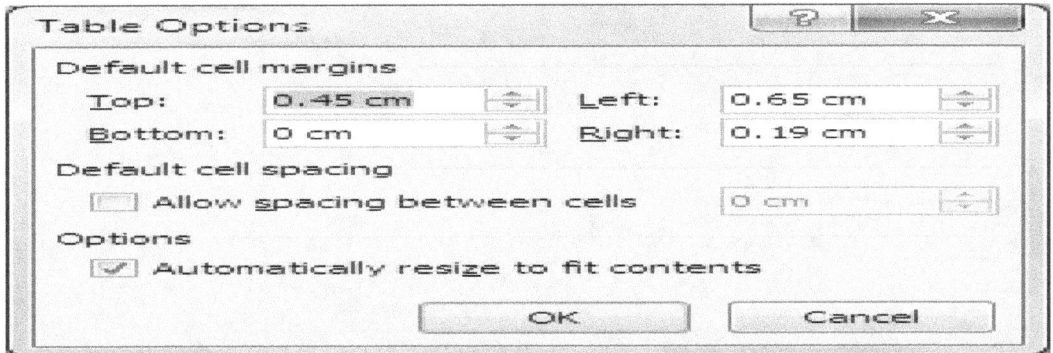

Sorting text in a table

You can sort text in tables in alphabetical order, you can also chose which columns should be sorted first. For example first sort column 1 that contains the surname and then by column 2 that contains the firstname.

Ascending order will sort data from a to z and descending order will sort data from Z to A

Sorting by column 1 and then by column 2

- Click on the down arrow next to the word column 1 if you wish to change the sort order

Move the cursor to the Then by, down arrow and select column 2 to be the second sort oder

Sorting in Ascending order

- Click inside the little round circle next to the word ascending, a blue dot must appear inside the dot to indicate that the option has been selected

Header row

If your table has headings for example the words name, surname and telephone number appear in the first row of a telephone list, we will indicate that the list has a header row, since if we don't the header row will also be sorted in alphabetical order

- Click inside the table, click on sort, click inside the little square to create a V inside the square to indicate that the table has a header row

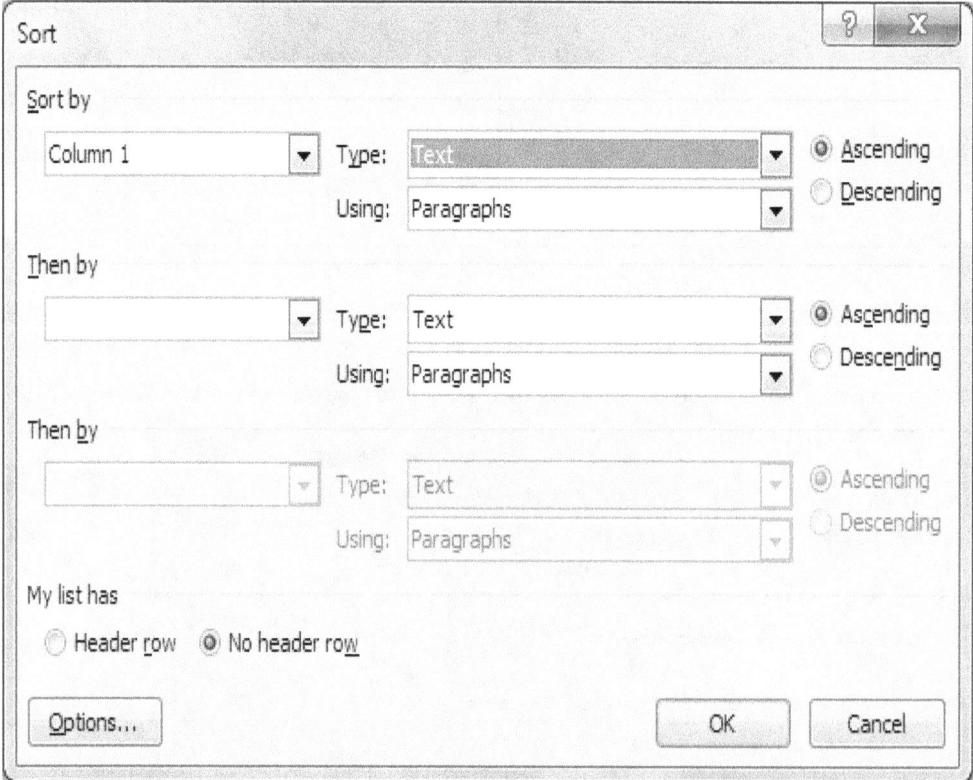

Microsoft Word 2010 Training Manual level 2

Inserting pictures and objects 60 min

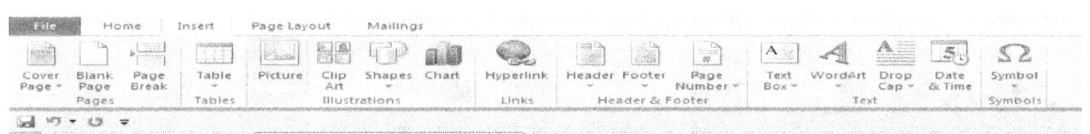

Insert symbol

You can insert any symbol that is not on your standard keyboard

> Click on insert, symbol, select the item that you want

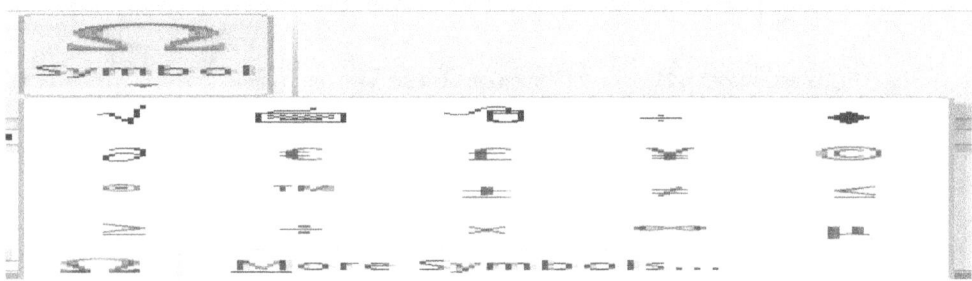

> Click on more symbols, to select other symbols

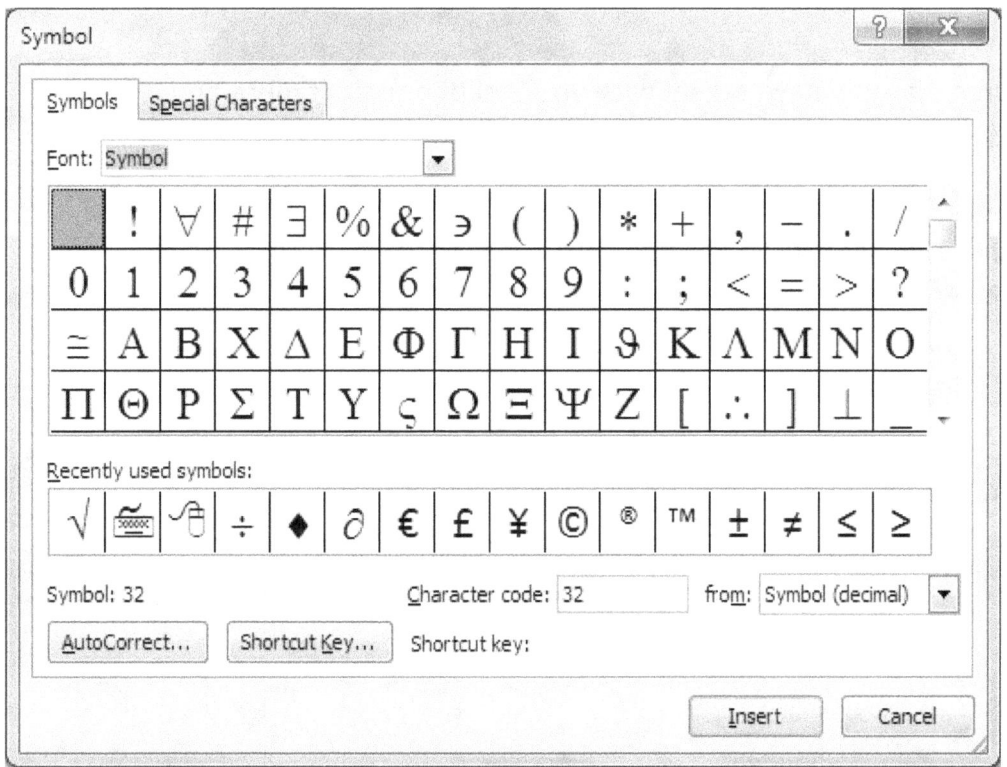

Change the font, to wingding to view more pictures, by clicking on the down arrow

Click on the ☺smiley face and click on insert to insert a smiley face into your document

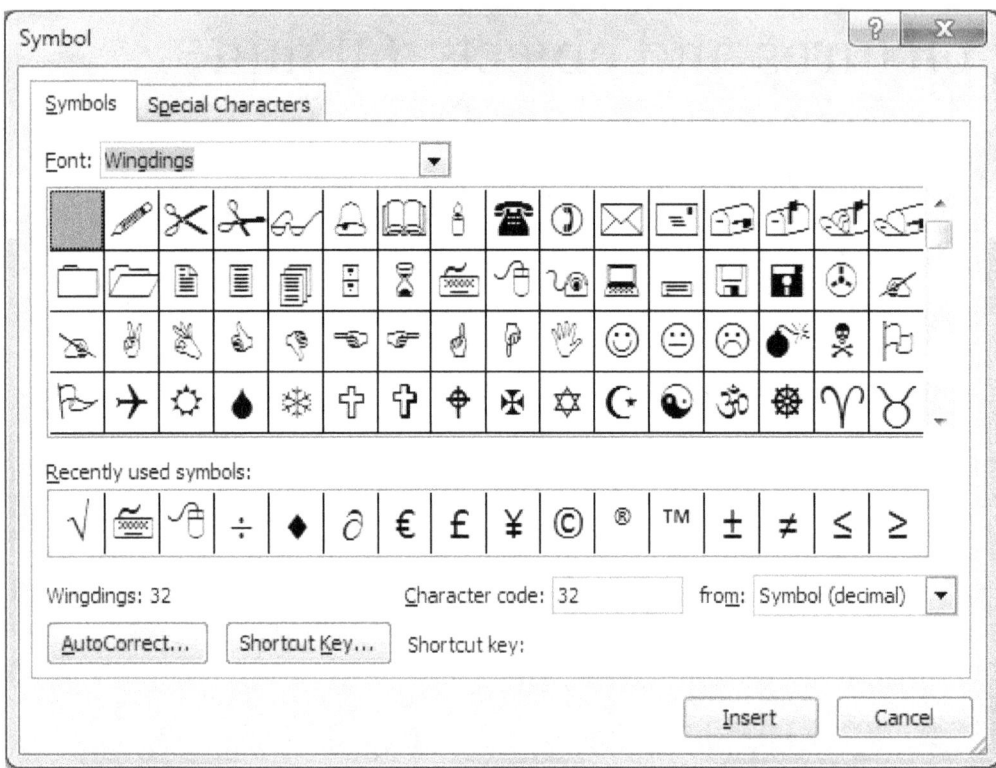

Inserting a picture

You can add pictures that you have taken with your cellphone or camera and insert it into MS Word

- ➢ Click on insert picture
- ➢ Click on the folder where the picture is located
  You will have to transfer the pictures from your camera or cellphone to your computer

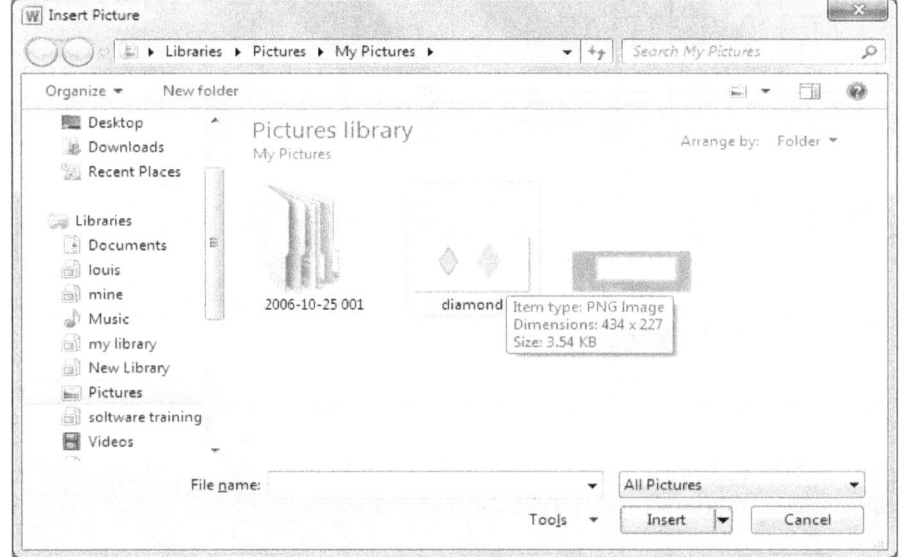

➢

The picture above is not part of the Microsoft clip art gallery; it is a picture that I have taken.

Insert clip art

Clip art is a list of pictures that Microsoft has made that you can add into your document

The Clip art options will appear on the right side of the screen.

At the search for option:

- Click on the <go> button to list all pictures from clip art or

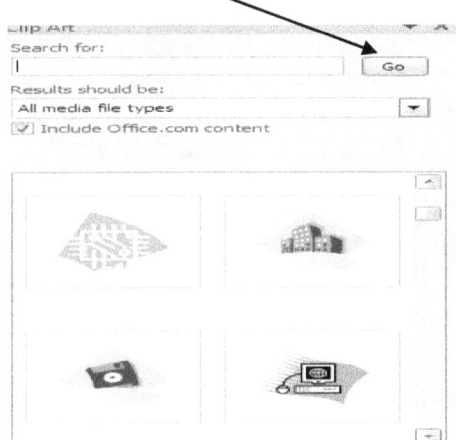

Click on the up and down arrow of the scroll bar to scroll through the different pictures that are available.

- Or Type in the name of a picture that you want to search for and click on <go>

Practise exercise: search picture: at the search option type in <car>, A list of cars will apear,

- click on the picture you want to add to your document

Insert shape

There are different type of objects/ shapes you can insert into a Microsoft word document

- Click on insert shape,
- Select the shape you wish to add to your document
- How to draw the picture inside the document
    - Position the cursor at the starting point and
    - Press down the left button on the mouse, don't release the mouse buton and
    - Drag the cursor to the right and down to create the shape

There are many different shapes to choose from:

Changing pictures and objects

Making pictures bigger or smaller

Once the picture is selected, little round circle's appear around the picture, this is your resize buttons, by positioning the cursor on one of the circles you can drag the picture smaller or bigger. The green circle will turn the picture in the direction of your choice

- Click on the object to select it
- Click on the little white circle and drag it to the right to enlarge it
- Click on the little white circle and drag it to the left to make it smaller

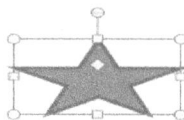

Formatting pictures

You can make changes to the formatting of the picture and add some nice frames around it

➢ Double click on the picture to activate the picture menu

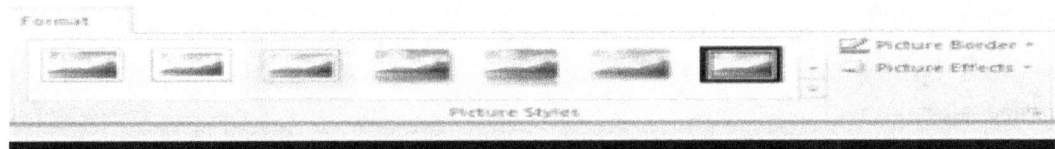

There are a list of picture frame styles you can use or you can create your own

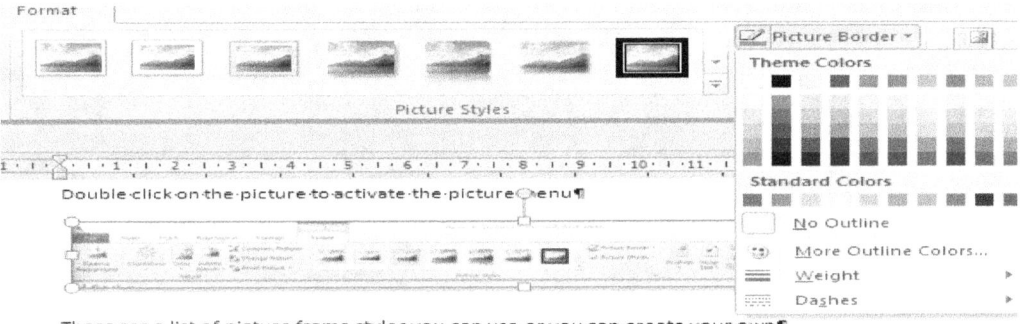

Insert Chart

You can create a Microsoft Excel chart and insert it into MS Word

➢ Click on <insert chart> the MS Excel program will open with the chart template

➢ Change the data that exist and add your information into the spreadsheet.

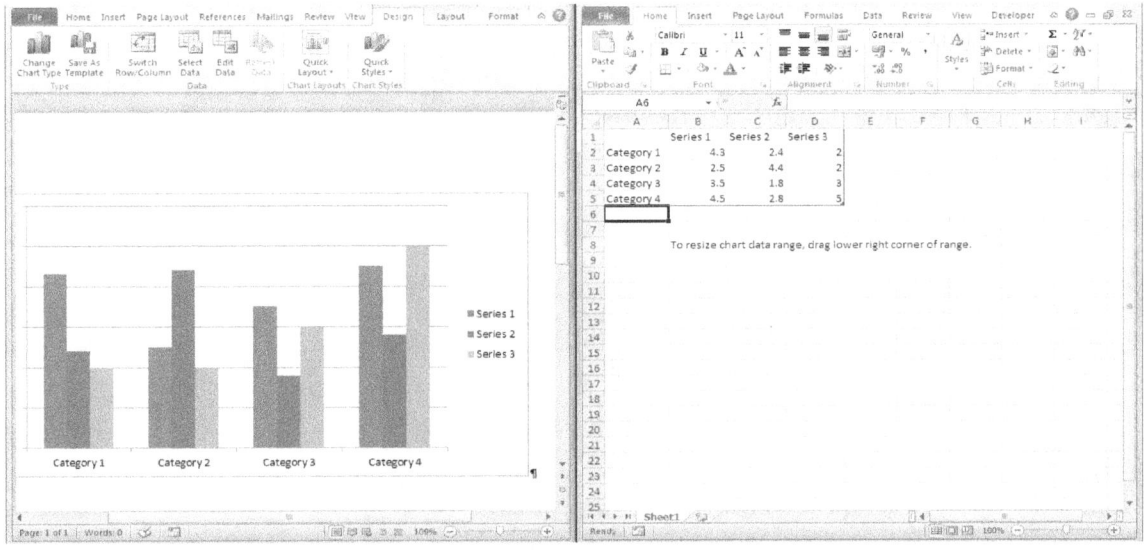

Another way of inserting a chart is to copy an Excel chart and paste it into MS Word:

Linking word and Excel   60 min

You can copy and paste existing Excel sheets into word.

The data link option is activated when you paste the data, this means your data will be updated.

- ➢ Go to Excel, select copy
- ➢ Go to word and select paste

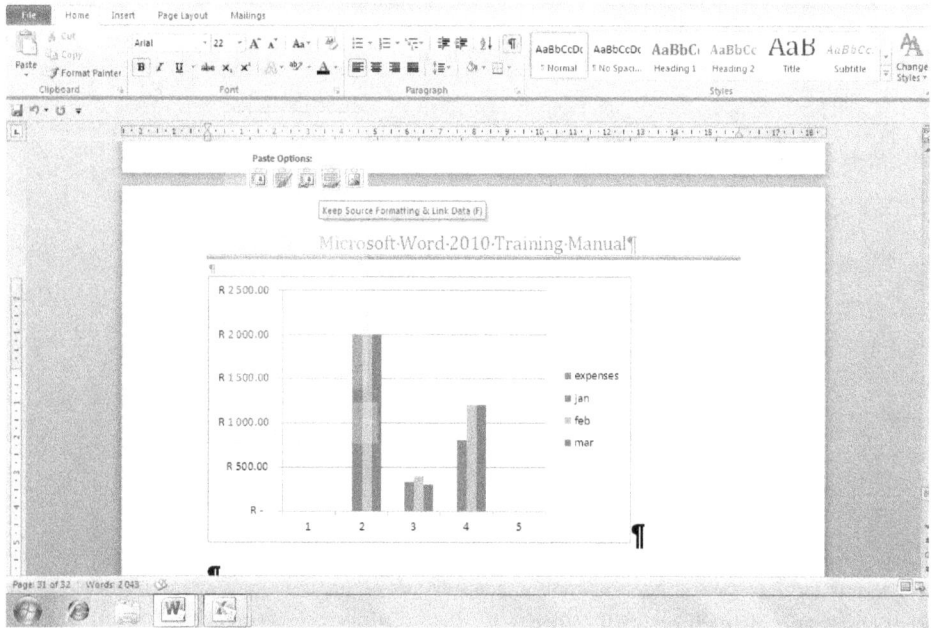

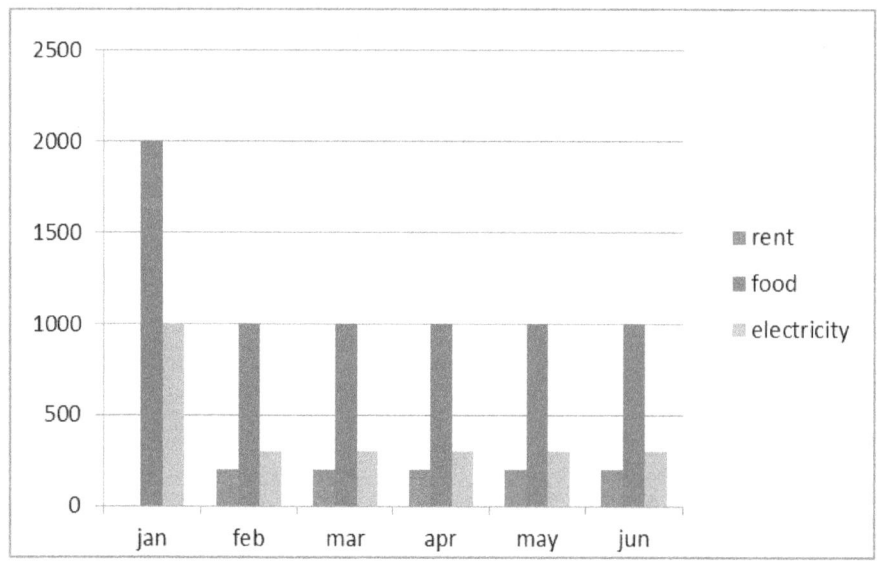

Microsoft Word 2010 Training Manual level 2

Headers and footers   30 min

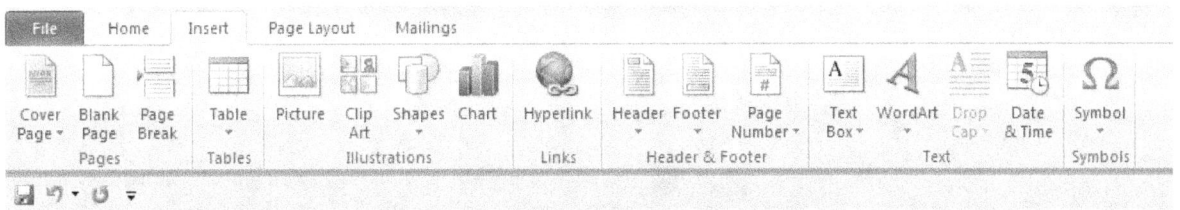

A header or footer is data that will repeat at the top or bottom of your document, you can also insert page numbers to your header or footer. Headers will insert data that will repeat at the top of the document. Footers will insert data at the bottom of the document to repeat.

Microsoft has header and footer templates that you can choose from.

- Click on insert, header or footer

- Click on the header or footer you wish for your document to activate header or footers

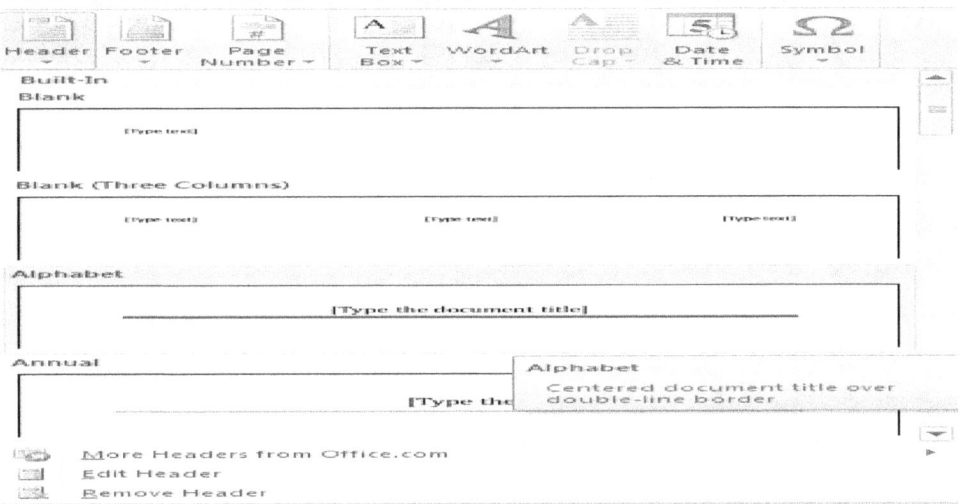

- Click on close header and footer when finished designing the header and footer

Notice at the bottom of the page, the footer

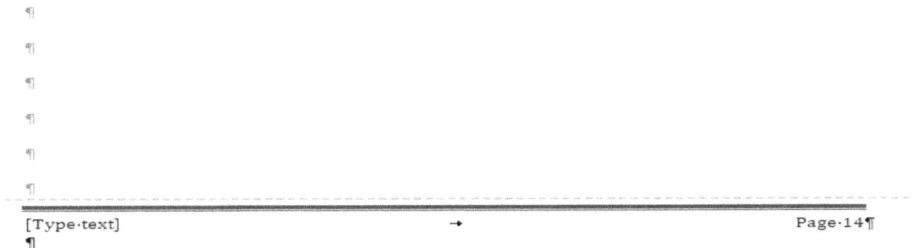

Microsoft Word 2010 Training Manual level 2

Page layout   30 min

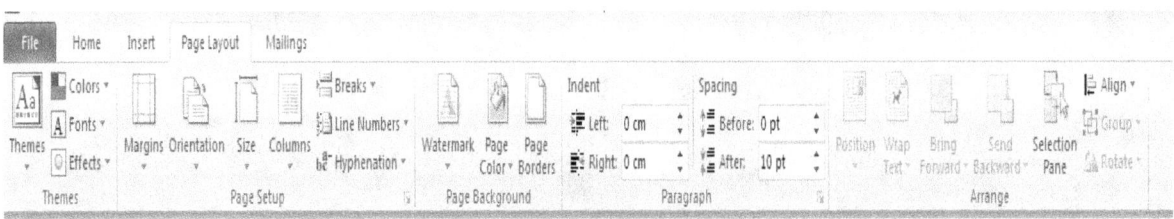

Themes

Instead of formatting your own document you can apply a set of formatting to your document.

A document theme is a set of formatting choices that include a set of theme colors, a set of theme fonts (including heading and body text fonts), and a set of theme effects (including lines and fill effects)

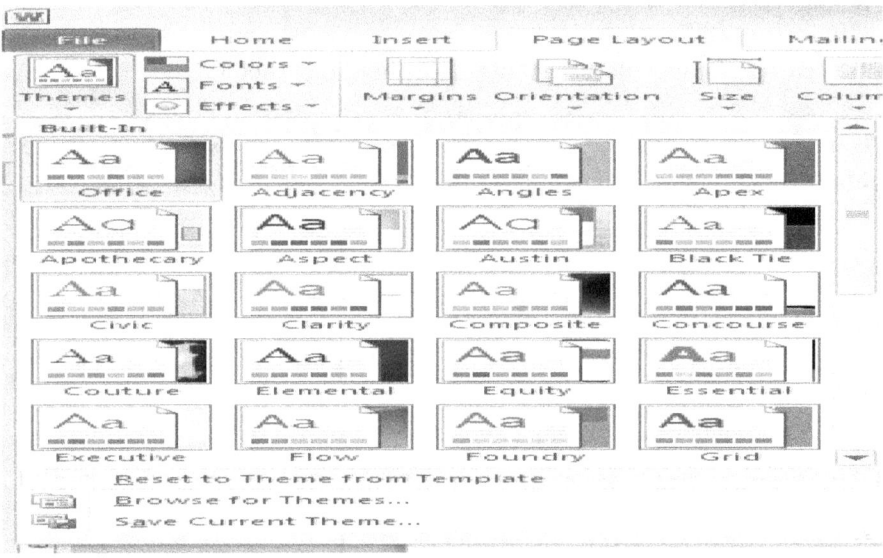

Margins

You can change the top left bottom and right margins in page layout

> Click on custom margin and change the margins to your choice

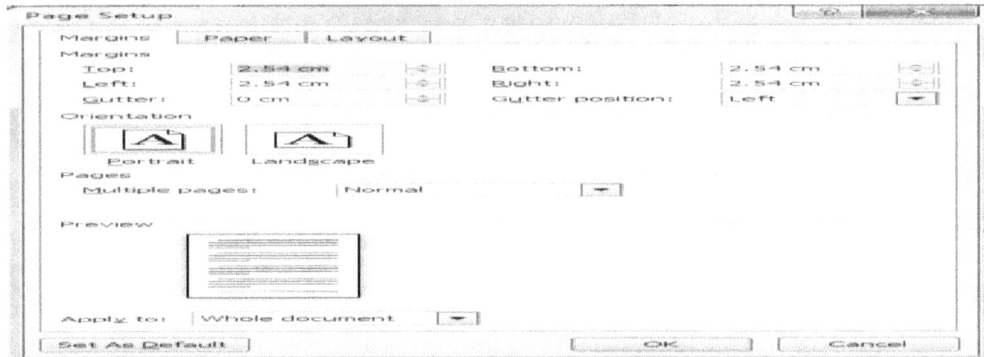

Orientation

You can change the page layout to portrait or landscape. Most word documents are printed out in portrait view.

Size

You can change the size of the document to a4 or a5 , a3,a6 or any of the options available or create a custom size

Columns

You can change your page layout to divide your data into 2 or three columns on default you work only in one column.

If you wish to apply more than one format on a page you must insert a section break

Below is a sample of 3 columns

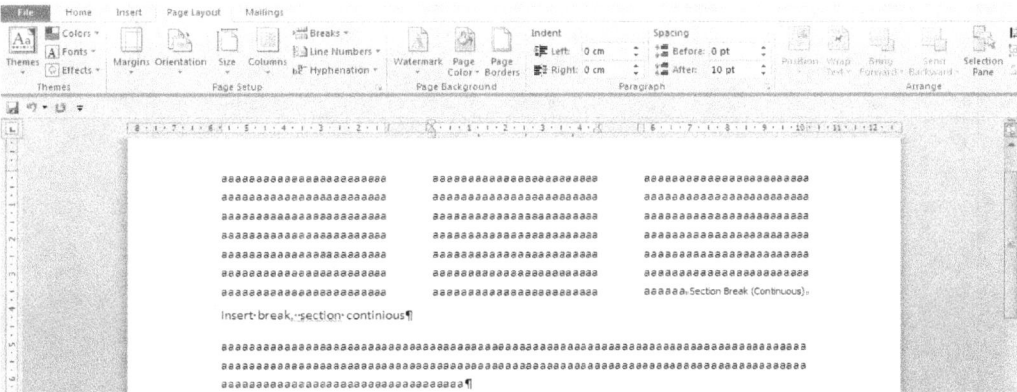

Breaks

Inserting **page breaks** will allow the data to be placed on the next page.

Inserting a **continues section break** will allow you to change the format and apply different formats onto one page

Inserting a section break

A section break is needed when you like in example above want to apply different column formats onto one page

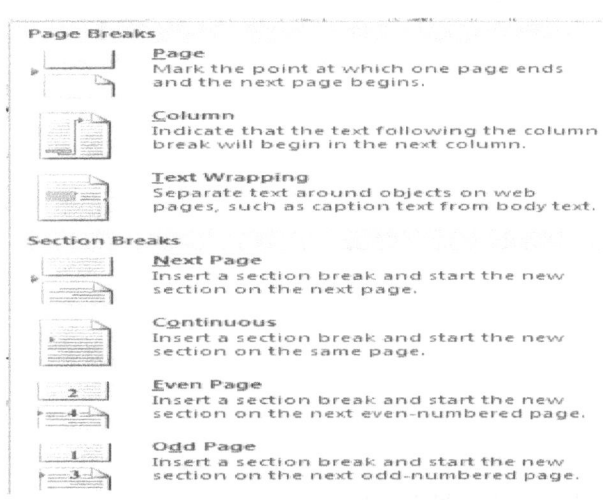

- Click on page layout
- Click on breaks
- Click on section break continuous

Formatting columns

You can decide what the width of the columns will be and how large the space between the columns will be and you can create a vertical line between the columns

> ➤ Click on page layout, click on the down arrow underneath the word column, the column dialog box will appear:

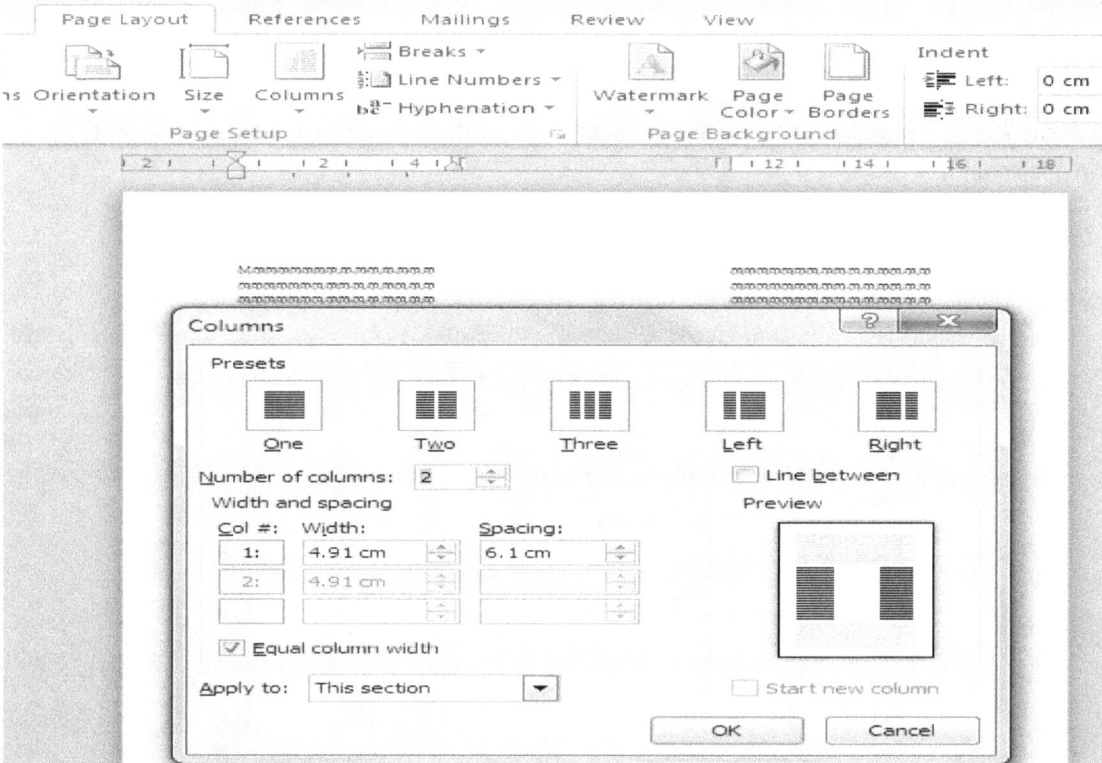

Changing the width of the columns

- o Click on the down arrow underneath the word width and specify the column width

Changing the spacing between the columns

- o Click on the up or down arrow underneath the word spacing and specify the spacing

Creating a line between the columns

On the left side of the word <line between> is a small square

> ➤ Click inside the little square to produce a √, which indicate that a vertical line will be drawn between the columns

Removing the vertical line between columns

> ➤ Click inside the little square that has a √, which indicate that a vertical line will be drawn between the columns, clicking NOW inside the column, will remove the √, which means that the vertical line will not be drawn

Microsoft Word 2010 Training Manual level 2

Watermark

A watermark will allow text of your choice in the background of the document

- ➢ Click on page layout, Watermark

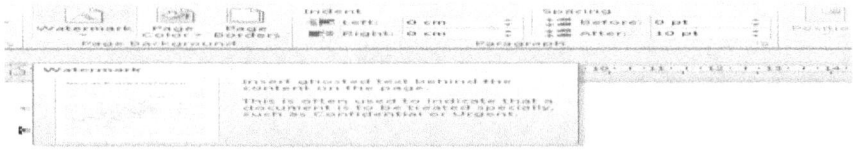

Page color

You can change the page color of your document
- ➢ Click on page layout, Page color, click on the color of your choice.

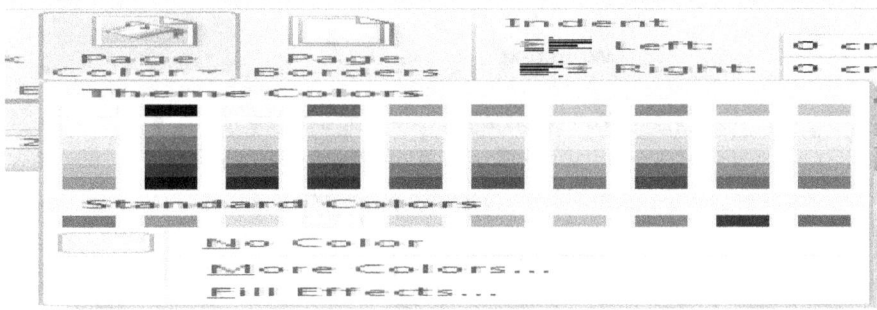

Page border

You can put a borderline around your page by defining the colour, and style of the lines for the border that will be around your page

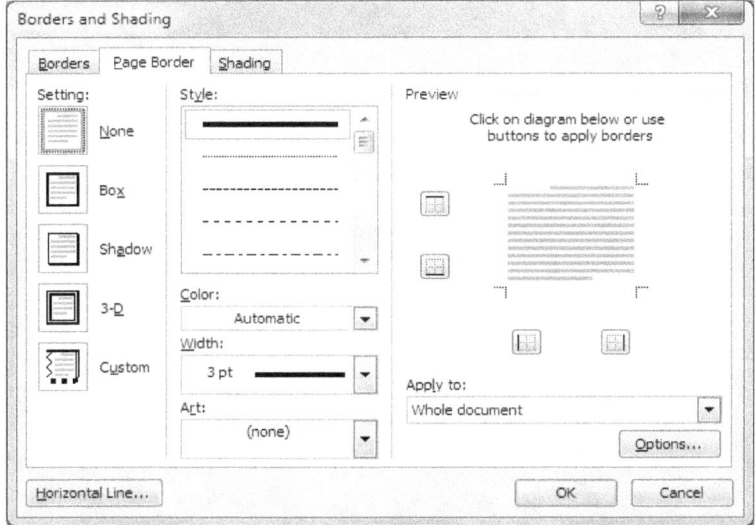

Microsoft Word 2010 Training Manual level 2

Position

You can choose to position your picture Inline with text or wrap text around picture

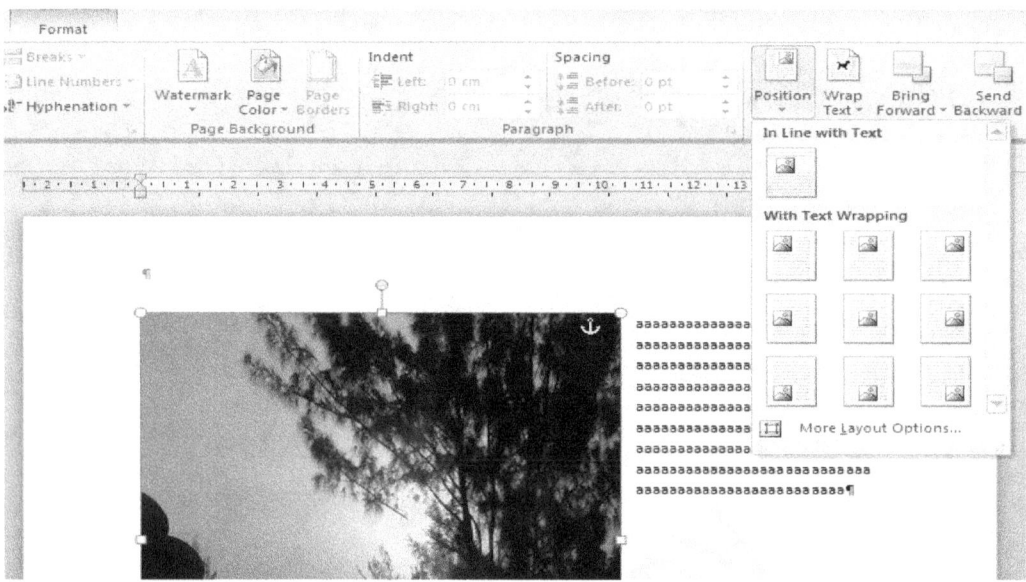

Wrap text

You can choose where and how your picture will appear on the screen and how it will interact with your text

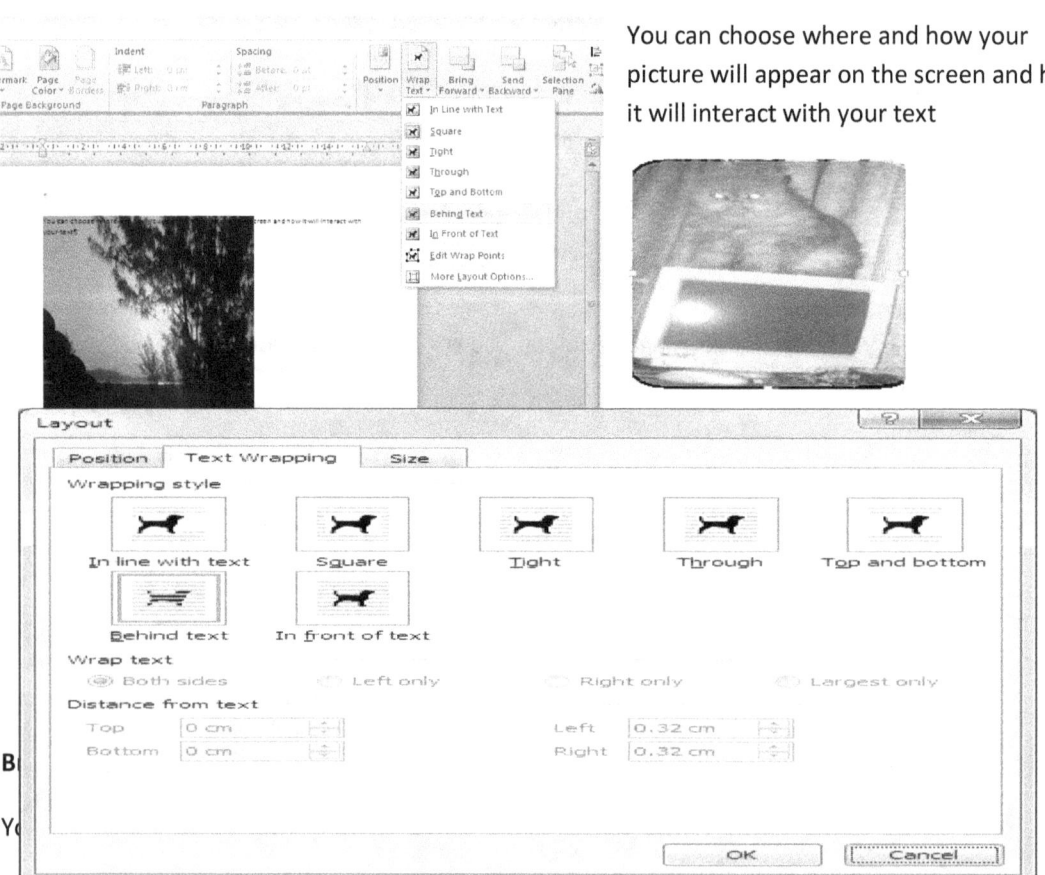

Send backward

You can send the picture behind the text

Selection pane

Activating the selection pane you can view all your pictures on the right side of the screen

- ➤ Click on a picture to make the picture formatting menu above available,

- ➤ and click on <selection pane>

    The selection pane should now be visible on the right side of the screen, listing all the picture names

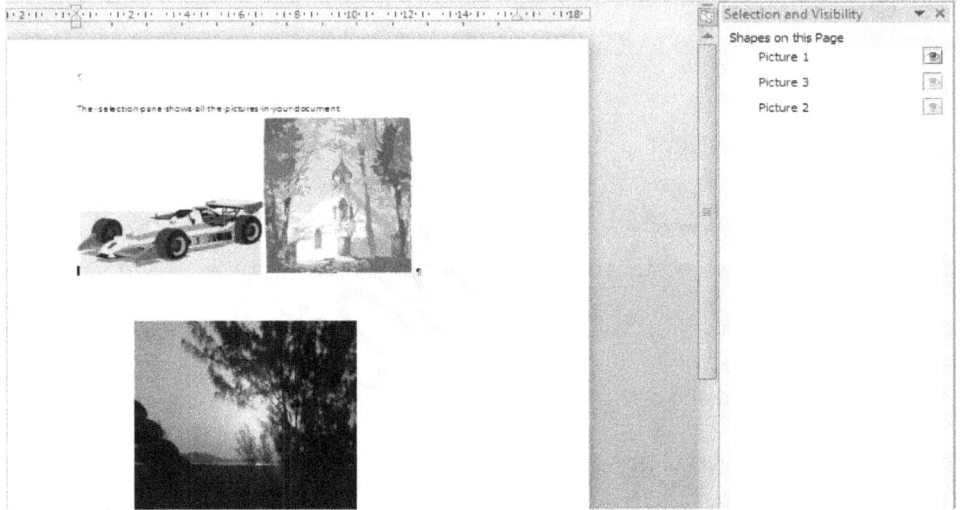

Aligning

You can align your pictures to the right left or centre

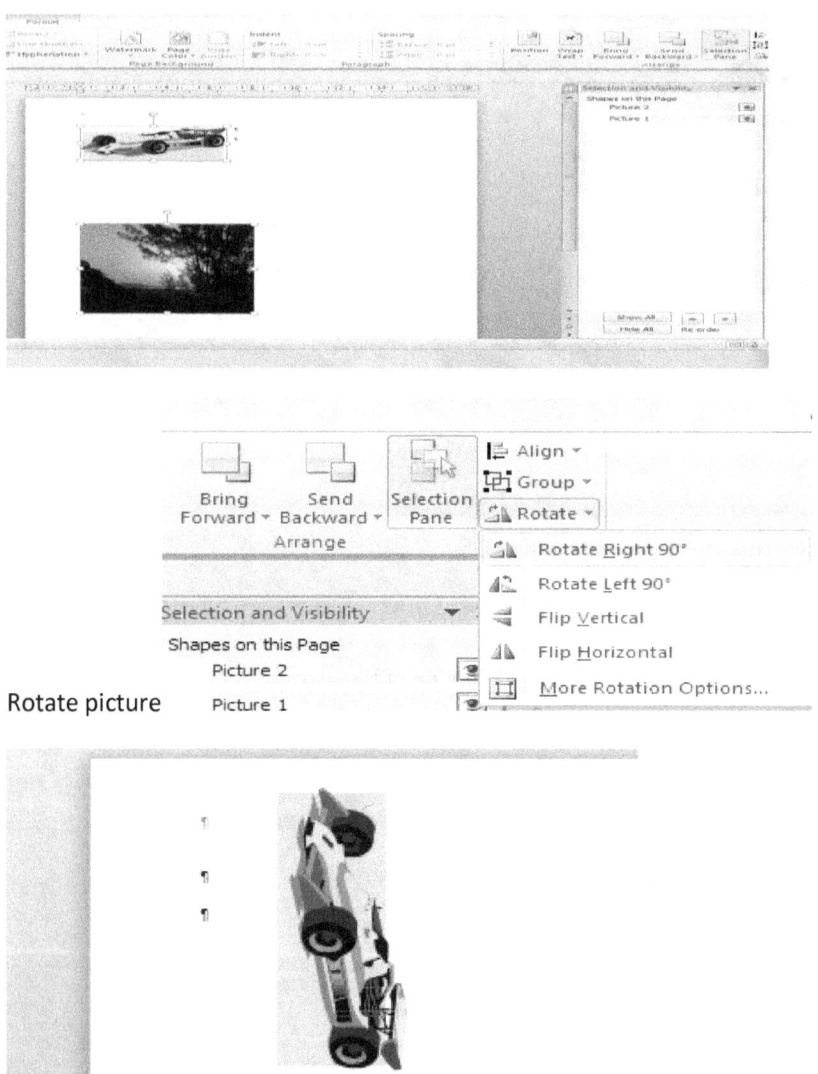

Rotate picture

Group objects

When grouping objects it means they will be addressed as one unit, thus if you wish to move a picture that is grouped to another object, the object that are grouped will move with it.

How to group:

Hold down the control button on the keyboard and click on all the objects that must be grouped.

- ➢ Click on the group button to group these items

- ➢ Click on the ungroup option to ungroup these items

Microsoft Word 2010 Training Manual level 2

Templates

Templates are documents that already has formatting and data in and you can use them to add data.

Usually templates are created for company documents and faxes and invoices.

Microsoft has a few templates that are created that you can use and you can also create your own templates.

How to use existing templates

- Click on file new
- Select the template you want to use
- Click on create

How to create your own template

- Go to Microsoft word
- Type in the letter and format it
- When saving the document, save it as document type <template>

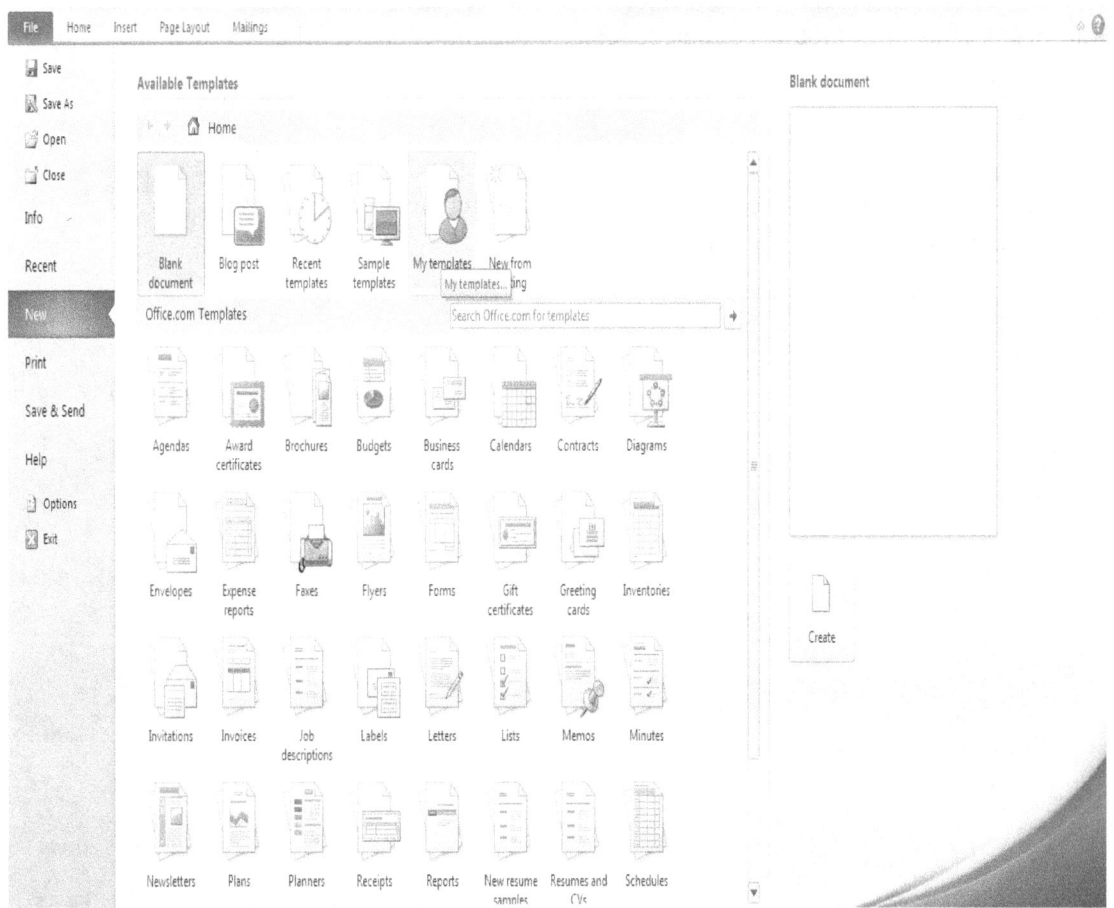

Microsoft Word 2010 Training Manual level 2

Saving documents

When saving documents you can save it as a different file type. Microsoft word saves your documents as a MS Word(doc) extension 2010 version.

Saving to a previous version

Select word 97 to 2003 if you wish to view these documents on an earlier version

Earlier version cannot read the 2010 format, or save it as a pdf or xps file

Pdf(portable document format)

You can save your word document into a pdf format which means anyone can read the document with adobe reader., thus other people don't need MS Word to read the document.

Pdf also protects your work ,since users can read the data and browse through the document and cannot make changes to your document when they are using adobe reader.

Once you save it to pdf format, you cannot change it back to MS Word format.

XPS

This is also a document reader format ,once you saved it to xps format you cannot change it back to doc. Xps is platform independent and you will be able to read word documents even when you don't have MS Word.

Txt

If you want to use notepad to open your document ,then save it to txt format, however many of your formatting will be lost when you save to this format.

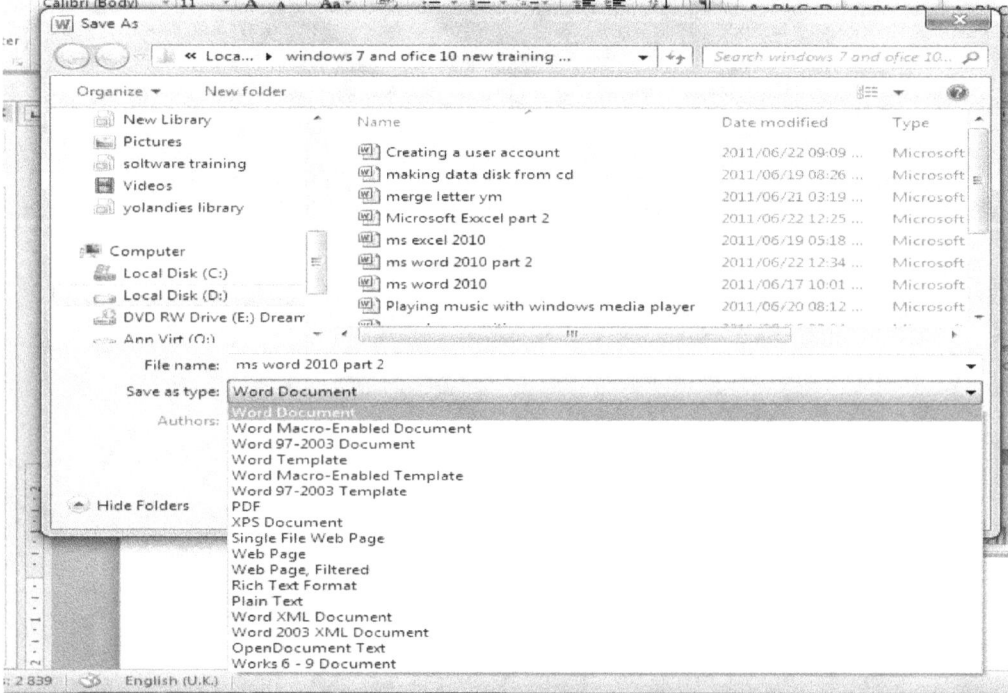

Microsoft Word 2010 Training Manual level 2

Changing MS Word settings

You can change many of the MS Word settings

- Click on File < options>

   The following screen appears:

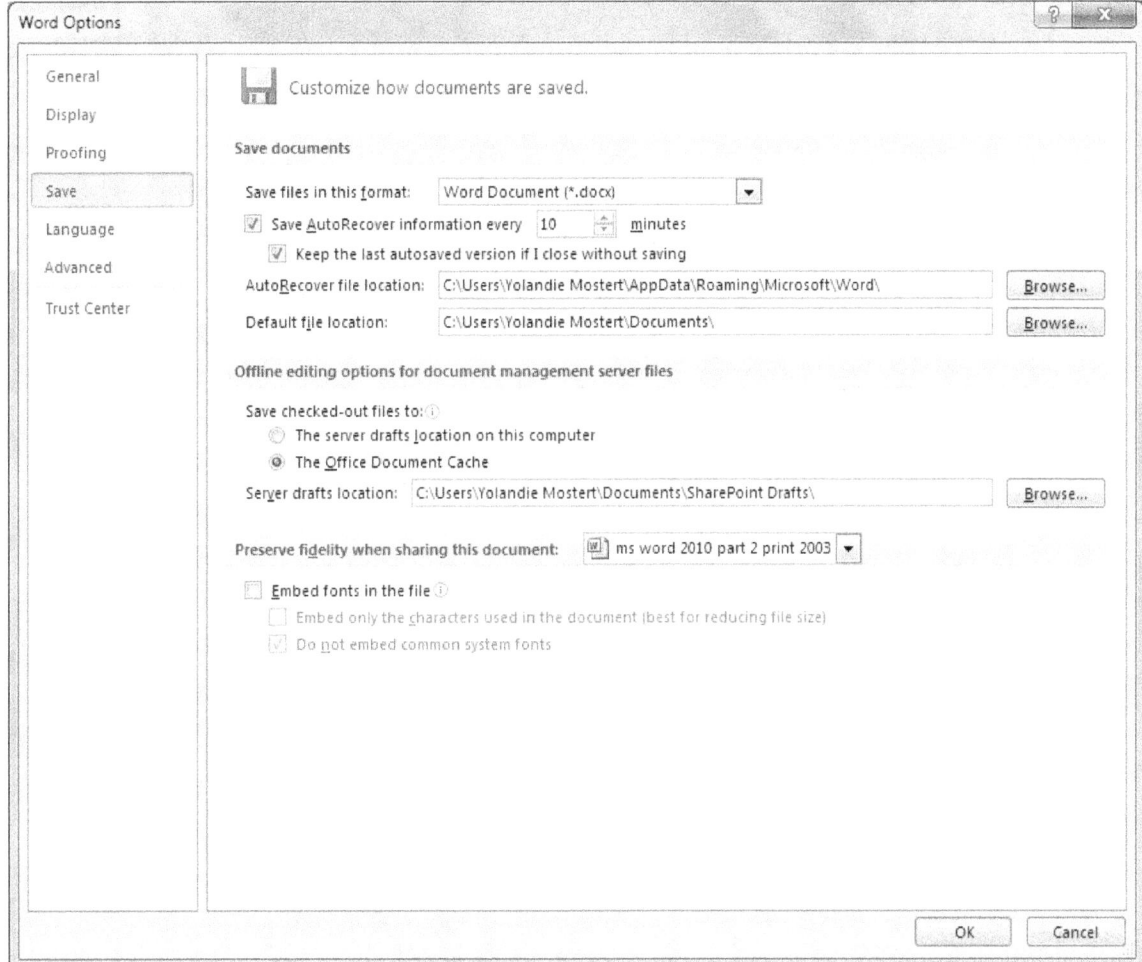

Autocorrect

Autocorrect is a special feature that type in words for you in the document or correct certain spelling in words as you type. You can also create your own autocorrect words

To change the autocorrect options

- Select proofing
- Click on autocorrect options

   a list of all the autocorrect options will apear

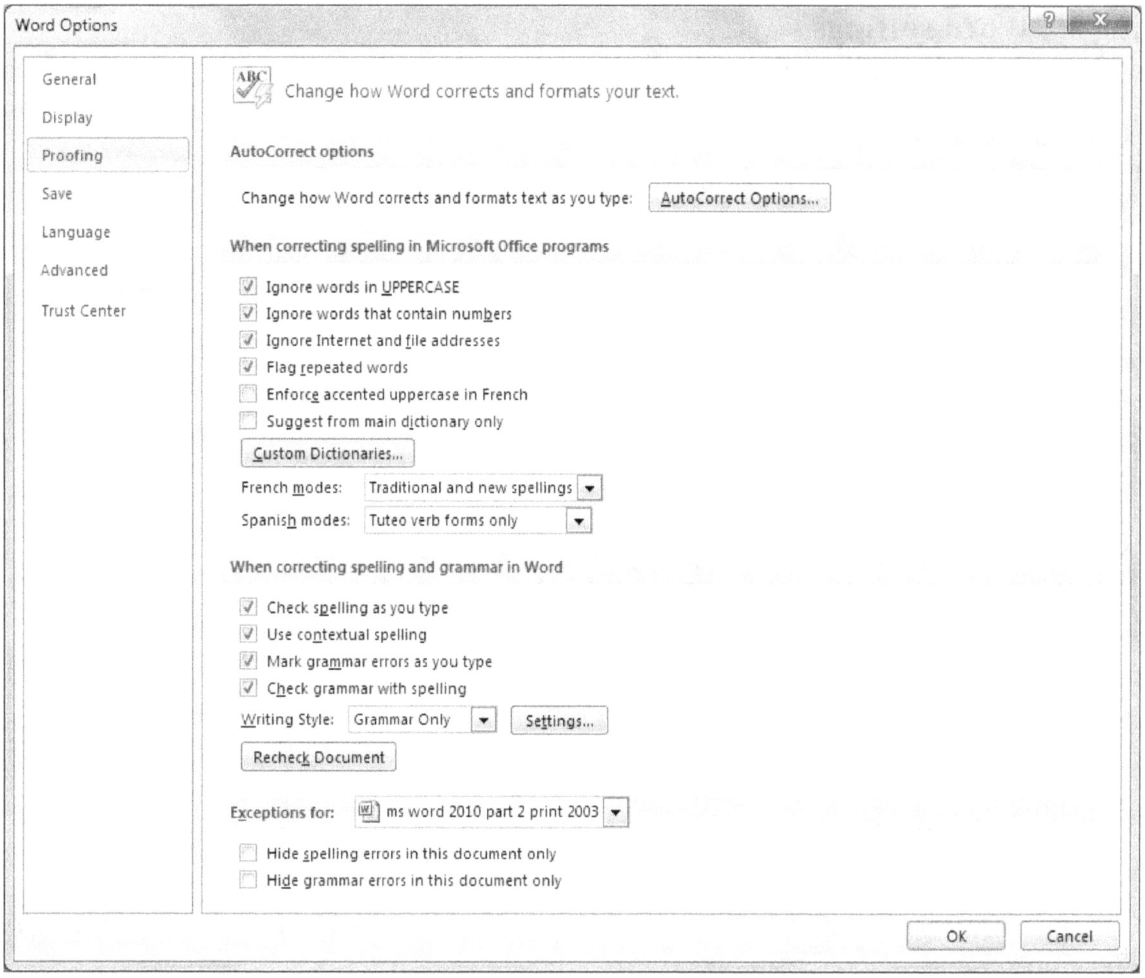

Microsoft Word 2010 Training Manual level 2

>

Exercise creating new autocorrect entry:

> Type in the word <yol> to be replaced with the word Yolandie

> Click on add

Every time you type in the word yol it will be replaced with the word

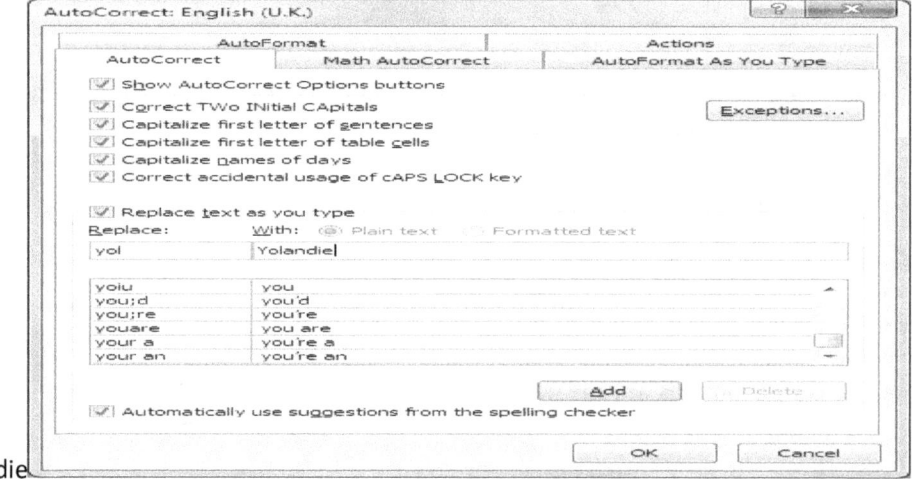

Yolandie

Translating words to French

On the upper right corner of the menu

- Click on the down arrow underneath the spelling option
- Click on <Translate selected text>
- Click on the option <translate>
- In the search for option box:
- Type a word you want to translate to French or highlight a word in your document
- Press the green right arrow next to the word that will be translated

Make sure that the word translation is viewable underneath the search for option and

Make sure that <from> English <to> Frensch is selected

Translating words to Spanish

On the upper right corner click on the down arrow underneath the spelling option

- Click on the option <translate>
- Click on Translate selected text
- In the search for option box:
- Type a word you want to translate to spanish or highlight a word in your document
- Press the green right arrow next to the word that will be translated

Make sure that the word translation is viewable underneath the search for option and Make sure that <from> English <to> spanish is selected

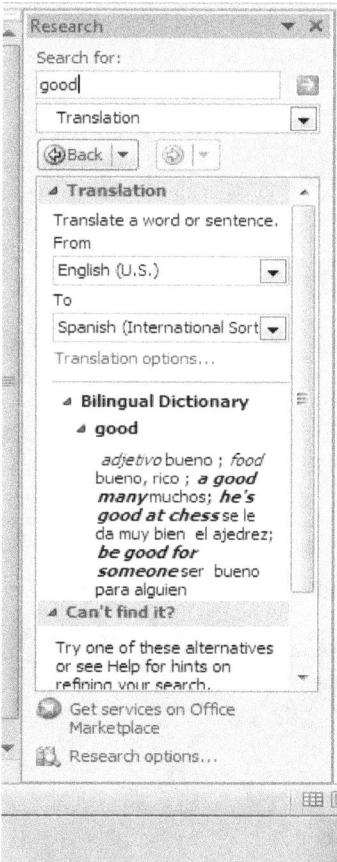

Advanced printing

Activate the print preview option to first preview documents before printing

- Click on printer , print properties
- Select print preview by clicking inside the little square box at the preview before print option

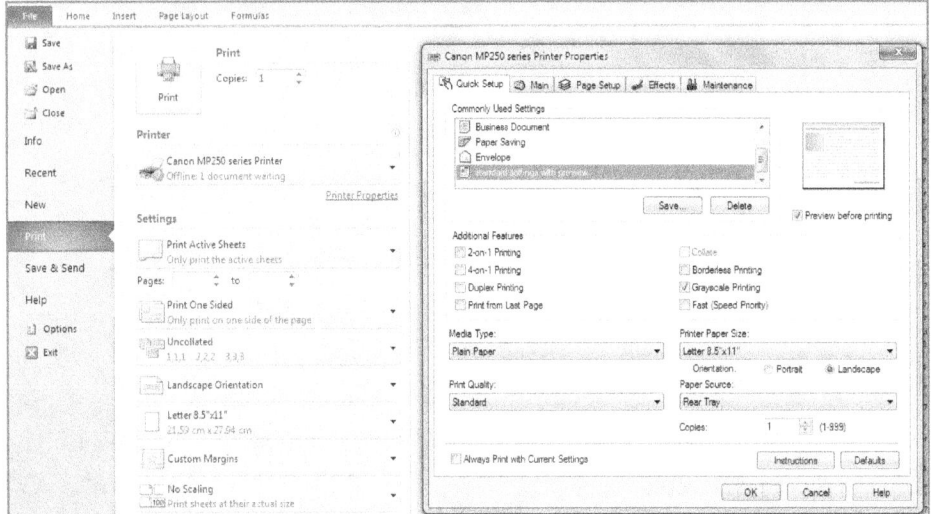

When satisfied with the preview, click on start printing

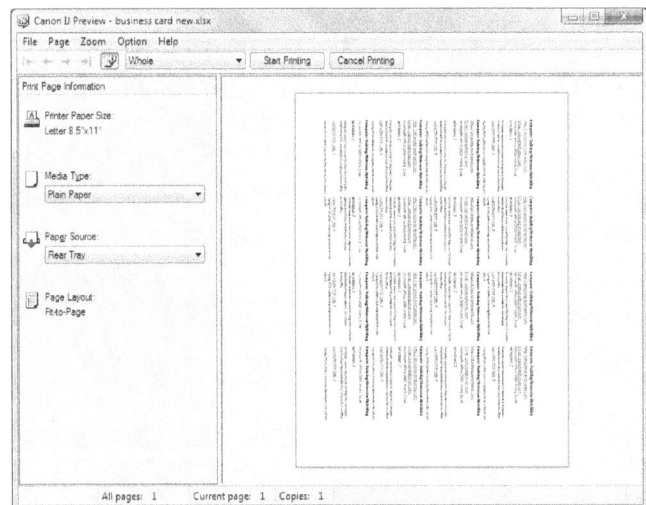

If the printer is not connected the following screen will appear

Click on display print queue to check which documents are scheduled to be printed

Microsoft Word 2010 Training Manual level 2

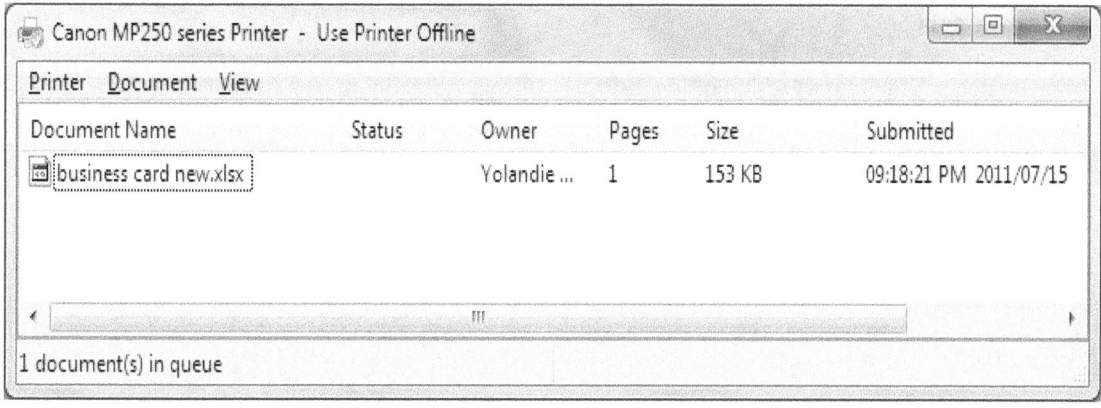

To open the print queue while it is connected:

- Click on Control panel, hardware and sound, devices and printers and
- click on the printer's name.
   the print queue will open and the jobs scheduled to be printed will be listed

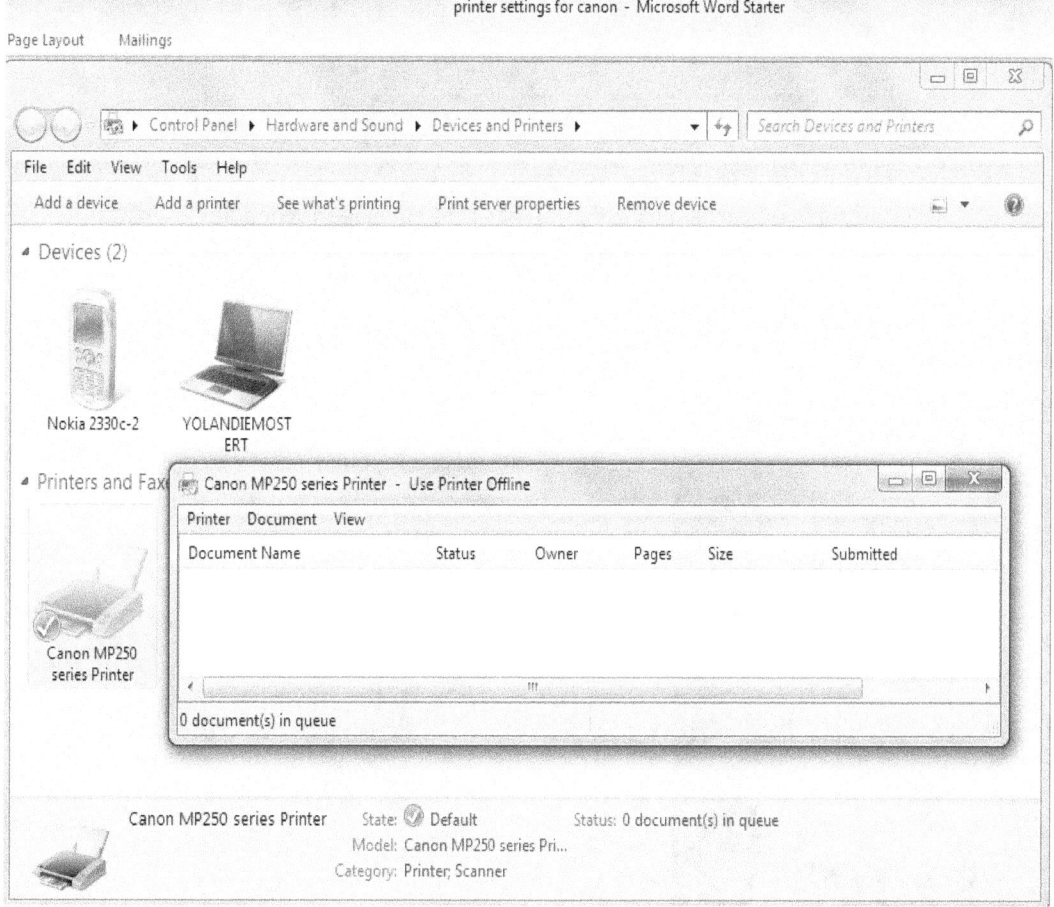

View when document is scheduled to print

- Click on the document name in the print queue
- Select <document> on the print queue menu
- Click on properties

The following screen will appear

It will list whether the document is set as a high or low priority. Setting a document as a high priority will allow it to be printed before other documents in the queue. It also indicated what time the document is scheduled to be printed.

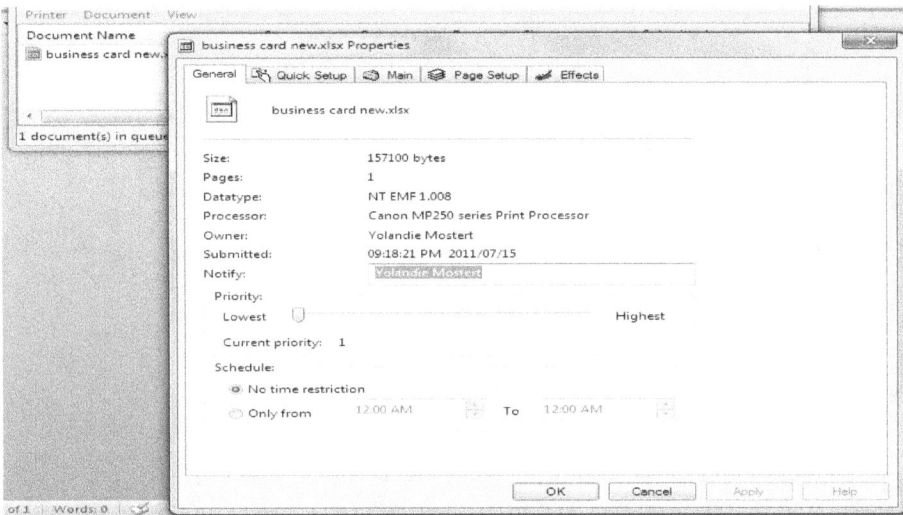

Cancelling printing.

After you have pressed the print button, you can still cancel print jobs that have been scheduled to print

- Click on printer
- Click on cancel all documents
- Click on <yes> cancel print when prompted

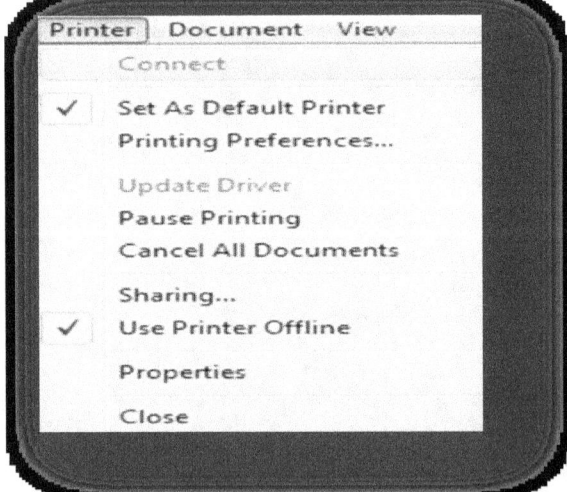

---

i This is an example of an endnote, end notes appear at the end of the document

This is the end of this training manual, for more books please visit these websites:

Word level 3 is currently available at a discounted price.

Order your copy today at QualityTraining.Yolasite.com and have your digital(PDF) copy immediately downloaded to your computer

For more interesting reading Goto www.lulu.com/spotlight/worldpeace734

Thank you for your support, each book you purchase will provide funds to help/ educate poor people and some funds will also be used to feed hungry animals

www.ingramcontent.com/pod-product-compliance
Lightning Source LLC
Chambersburg PA
CBHW080848170526
45158CB00009B/2675